A Collection of
Jujutsu Manuals
Volume III

Jujutsu Books from:

1600-1868   1868-1912   1912-1926
E d o · Meiji · Taisho

Translated by Eric Shahan

CW00688737

COPYRIGHT © 2021 ERIC MICHAEL SHAHAN
ALL RIGHTS RESERVED.
ISBN: 978-1-950959-42-6
IMPRINT: ERIC MICHAEL SHAHAN

Translator's Introduction

- *An Illustrated Guide to Kenpo* (Edo Era)
  This chapter has Tengu mountain goblins introducing Muto Dori, or fighting unarmed against an armed opponent. These techniques are likely from the Yoshin School.

- *Hokusai's Manga* (Edo Era)
  These sketches by the famous master illustrator give an insight into how Jujutsu and other fighting arts were practiced. His illustrations clearly show the application of joint locks.

- *How to Treat Victims of Drowning or Hanging* (1878)
  This is a police manual that uses Jujutsu striking points to revive victims of accidental or intentional hanging or drowning.

- *Fundamentals of Military Strategy: An Illustrated Guide to the Secrets of Jujutsu, Kenjutsu and Bojutsu* (1887)
  Part 2 of this translation contains 10 standing techniques from the Tenjin Shinyo Ryu Jujutsu School.

- *The Fundamentals of Jujutsu : A Study in Physical and Psychological Development* (1909)
  A short introduction to Jujutsu training. This pamphlet was probably an advertisement.

- *Free Sparring, Resuscitation & Jujutsu Textbook* (1912)
  Part 1 of a very interesting Jujutsu book that contains a complete training system. This the same author as *Fundamentals of Military Strategy*, though he changed his name.

Notice and Caution! This work is being translated for historical research purposes to study the development of resuscitation techniques in Japan and how they are connected to Jujutsu. It should not be considered a lifesaving guide. It should not be considered to be an instruction manual. Do not attempt to use, employ or try any of these techniques.

ERIC SHAHAN シャハン・エリック

Kenpo Zu
An Illustrated
Guide to Kenpo

Part 2: Muto

Copied by
Fujita Seiko

Date Unknown
Edo Era

Translator's Introduction to Tengu Part 2

Kenpo Zu, An Illustrated Guide to Fighting, is a series of 59 images of Tengu, mountain goblins, engaged in combat. While Tengu are often depicted as tricksters they also are credited with teaching the sword arts to many famous Samurai over the course of Japanese history.

Tengu are a type of Yokai, or supernatural being. The two Kanji that make up this word are "sky" and "dog" which recalls the earlier Chinese meaning of the word, a constellation or a celestial event, such as a comet, that was considered a harbinger of ill fortune. In Japan, the first mention of Tengu as a celestial event was in the 8th century, however by the 12th century the Tengu were seen as mischievous spirits that led Buddhist and Zen monks astray, particularly those that were prideful or lazy. They also attempted to misdirect average people by pretending to be the Buddha.

While there is no text, *An Illustrated Guide to Kenpo* may be from the Yoshin School 楊心流 "The School of the Willow Heart." It was one of the three most influential schools of Jujutsu in the Edo Era, along with Takenouchi School 竹内流 and Ryoi Shinto School 良移心当流. There is no information regarding when *An Illustrated Guide to Kenpo* was created though it was likely sometime in the Edo Era (1600 ~ 1868.) The illustrations were copied by Fujita Seiko (1898 ~ 1966,) the 14th heir to the Koga School of Ninjutsu and a famous martial arts researcher, from a book in his collection. Each technique consists of a single image, likely serving as a reference for those who studied this school.

Though there is no text in the book, the techniques seem to be divided into three categories:

- Jujutsu
- Muto (An unarmed opponent against another with a sword)
- Dueling with Weapons. This can be Katana vs Katana, Katana vs Jutte (truncheon) or Katana vs Tessen (metal fan)

An Illustrated Guide to Fighting contains 59 illustrations. *A Collection of Curious Jujutsu Manuals Volume II* introduced the 31 Jujutsu techniques. This volume will introduce the 23 Muto techniques. Muto, which translates directly as "no-sword," refers to any technique used for fighting an armed opponent while you are unarmed.

Jujutsu 31 Techniques	Muto 23 Techniques

Dueling with weapons 5 Techniques

The illustrations consist of two Tengu demonstrating Muto techniques. There is one Tengu with an Avian face and another with a human face, though it has an exaggerated nose. This long nose indicates the creature is a trickster. The winner of each technique alternates between the two Tengu. Though the winner is a different Tengu each time, they are always shown in darker clothing. Some illustrations show the victor holding a sword, however this indicates they took the sword at the end of the technique.

Muto translates literally to "No-sword" but more broadly means to fight an unarmed against an opponent who is armed. There are several famous episodes involving Muto techniques throughout history.

History of Muto

Most of the information regarding Muto techniques is from the Shin Kage "New Shadow" School.

Kamiizumi Nobutsuna

According to *Short Tales of Japanese Martial Bravery* 本朝武芸小伝 the sword saint and founder of the Shinkage "New Shadow" School, Kamiizumi Nobutsuna, developed Muto on a trip to Kyoto in 1563. He heard that an insane man had kidnapped a child and was hiding in a small hut with a sword. Kamiizumi went to Myōkōji Temple 妙興寺, shaved his head, borrowed a Kesa shawl from a priest and, now disguised as a travelling monk, entered the barn holding two rice balls. He offered the food to the deranged man, who reached for one.

The moment the man's attention was taken by the rice, Kamiizumi seized him and freed the child. The director Akira Kurosawa included this scene in the film Seven Samurai. Kamiizumi. Today Myokoji Temple is known as "the birthplace of Muto."

Yagyu Munetoshi

By 1594 Yagyu Munetoshi, who learned Shin Kage School from Kamiizumi had become quite well known. Tokugawa Ieyaseu, who, at the time was a general under Toyotomi Hideyoshi, invited Munetoshi to meet near Kyoto. Munetoshi agreed, and at the meeting explained the philosophy of his school and demonstrated some Kata including Muto techniques.

However Ieyasu wanted a better understanding of Muto, so he took up a Bokuto, wooden practice sword, and stood opposite Munetoshi requesting he demonstrate the technique on the general. Munetoshi sent Ieyasu's Bokuto flying and knocked the general to the ground. Ieyasu decided then to study the Shin Kage School.

Yagyu Munenori

Yagyu Munenori 柳生 宗矩 (1571 ~ 1646,) Munetoshi's son, had further developed Muto. There is a story of his prowess in *Japanese Tales of Sublime Martial Arts Volume 2* 日本武術神妙記. 続.

When the Daimyo Toyotomi Hidetsugu 豊臣秀次 (1568 ~1595) heard that Yagyu had travelled to Kyoto he invited him to his residence. When he arrived Toyotomi said, "I would like to see your Muto technique, which is quite famous."

Yagyu Munenori replied, "Muto is something you teach your students and encourage them to develop knacks to improve. It is not something I can adapt into a kind of amusement. So without holding a long or short sword to match my movements to, there is nothing I can show you."

Muto Technique

Yagyu Munenori wrote a chapter on Muto in *A Hereditary Book on the Art of War* 兵法家伝書, in 1732. The book contains three sections:
The Killing Sword
The Life-Giving Sword
Muto (No-Sword)

無刀之巻

The following is an excerpt from:
Muto Dori no Maki 1732 No-Sword Scroll
or
Fighting an Armed Opponent When You Are Unarmed Scroll

Do not attempt to take the sword away from an opponent committed to keeping his sword. If your opponent is committed to not letting his sword be taken, by not attempting to take it you are also doing Muto. For example, if you are facing an opponent who is only thinking, "I will not let my sword be taken, I will not let my sword be taken." You are confronting a person that has completely forgotten about trying to cut you and their attention will be focused solely on not having their sword taken. An adversary in that state of mind will not be able to cut another person. In our school, if you emerge from such an encounter without being cut, victory has been achieved. Muto is not the art of taking another person's sword. We train to develop Kufu, or knacks, to enable you to prevent the enemy from cutting you when you unarmed.

Muto, or fighting an armed opponent while you are unarmed, is not a technique for taking another person's sword. What it means is to make free use of any implement that may be around. If you, despite being unarmed, have the ability to take an opponent's Katana and use it against him, clearly you also have the ability to make use of some item you carry. Thus, you can use your folding fan to defeat an opponent holding a Katana. This approach to confrontation is the meaning of Muto. Say you are unarmed, but waking with a bamboo cane. You encounter an opponent who draws his sword and goes into a stance ready to strike. You can use your bamboo cane to take away his Katana. Even if you are unable to take his sword, you can still suppress his attack, meaning you do not get cut and thereby achieve victory. This way of thinking is the true meaning of Muto.

The purpose of Muto is not to take the opponent's sword way nor is it to cut the opponent. If your opponent has committed himself to cutting you down, you then have no choice but to seize his sword, however your initial purpose is not to steal his weapon.

It is necessary to develop the ability to discern your opponent's intent. What this means is you must develop the ability to discern if the Ma-ai, or distance between you and your opponent, is wide enough that even if he cuts, his sword will not reach you. If you clearly understand when you are out of reach of your opponent's attacks, you will not be afraid when he tries to cut you with his sword. If it seems like your opponent's attack will reach you, then you can judge the way his sword will move.

It is not possible to use Muto Dori, a technique for fighting unarmed against an armed opponent, if you are standing outside the range of the opponent's sword. In other words, your distance should be close enough so that his sword can cut you.

When doing Muto Dori, a no-sword technique, the opponent is holding a sword and you should think of yourself as fighting barehanded. Since your opponent has a long bladed weapon and you only have short hands, it is necessary to move close to the attacker. The important thing you need to understand is that this means that the battle is between the opponent's sword and your hands. Thus your body needs to maintain distance from your opponent's sword while you move towards the handle of his sword. Then you have to develop ways of moving that allow you to suppress his sword. However, you have to understand that each situation will be different and not follow a prescribed set of rules. No matter what the situation it is imperative that you move in so your body fits snugly against your opponent's.

Muto is the most secret technique in the Yagyu Shin Kage "New Shadow" School.

The way you hold your body, the way the opponent holds his sword, the field of battle, distance, the way you move your body, the way you move your feet, the opponent's stance, and the way the opponent is using his body and sword positioning to deceive you of his true intent are all part of Muto. These are the important points where you focus your attention.

An Illustrated Guide to Kenpo
Part II Muto
23 Techniques

Translator's Note: The Zen monk Takuan Soho also wrote about Muto. The following is an excerpt from his book :

The Mysterious Record of Immovable Wisdom (excerpt)
Takuan Soho (1573 ~ 1646)

The Buddhist Zen monk Takuan Soho, an acquaintance of Yagyu Munenori, wrote about Muto in his essay *The Mysterious Record of Immovable Wisdom.* He drew parallels between Buddhist thought and the arts of the warrior.

Takuan was born in the first year of Tensho (1573) in Tajima no Kuni (the northern part of present day Hyogo Prefecture) and devoted the whole of his life to the pursuit of Buddhism. He lived for Buddhism and fought for Buddhism.

When in Kanei 4 (1627) the Tokugawa Bakufu decreed that all appointments, Shugyo and promotions starting from the first year of Genwa (1615) at Myojinji Temple, Daitokuji Temple and so on, would be cancelled by order of the Emperor, he protested. Takuan insisted on the independence of Buddhism and defended their right to self-rule. Due to this at the age of fifty-six he was banished to Kami no Yama City in what is now Yamagata Prefecture. This is also known as the Shie Jiken, or the Purple Robe Incident referring to the purple robe worn by high level priests.

Friends of Takuan such as Yagyu Munenori and others appealed to the Shogun Iemitsu. Takuan who was the embodiment of Buddhist ideals greatly impressed Iemitsu who came to admire him and invite him to Edo.

In thanks to Yagyu Munenori, Takuan composed an essay that was later titled Fudo Chishin Myoroku, *The Mysterious Record of Immovable Wisdom.* Through Buddhism he lectured on the sword. Within his lecture on how the sword is a living thing he talked about how a person should prevail as a person, what they should do, he argued about what the ideal should be, and is overall credited with having a great influence on the establishment of Japanese Military Science and Martial Arts.

Fudochishin Myoroku (excerpt)
The Mysterious Record of Immovable Wisdom
By Takuan Soho

<ruby>無<rt>む</rt>明<rt>みょう</rt>住<rt>じゅう</rt>地<rt>う</rt>煩<rt>ち</rt>悩<rt>ぼんのう</rt></ruby>

むみょうじゅうちぼんのう
無明住地煩悩
Mumyo Juchi Bonno
Being Stopped by Polluting Thoughts Leads You Astray

The Kanji that make up the word Mumyo mean something that is unclear. It means that you are in doubt, hesitating and are unable to find enlightenment. The Kanji that make up the word Juchi (place you reside + ground) refer to a thing that takes hold of your mind. The Shugyo (intensive training) done in Buddhism is divided into fifty-two steps and hence it is called Goju Ni-i (fifty-two levels). The aforementioned Juchi is one of those levels. Juchi is anything that takes hold of the mind and keeps it prisoner. The first Kanji Ju means to stop (you stop in your home). What is meant by stop is that your mind has been stopped by something.

With regards to Kenjutsu if you, in the moment, the instant the enemy cuts with his Tachi join with it (As in thinking Ah! He is cutting!) you are focusing all your attention on the movement of the opponent's sword. By doing so you lose your own freedom of movement and you will be cut by the opponent. While you do, of course, see the enemy's Tachi you should in no way attempt to categorize and judge the opponent's cut and your own response. By not allowing your mind to stop on the opponent's raised sword and accepting the fact that the opponent's sword is striking, you will be able take the enemy's sword from his grasp and use it against him.

Within Zen this is known as Grabbing hold of the head of the spear that has been thrust at you and stabbing the person who attacked you. While the Kanji is the one for spear it actually refers to a Halberd in this case. What this means is that you can pluck the Katana out of the opponent's hands and reversing the situation, cut them down. Within Kenjutsu this is known as Muto Dori (fighting unarmed against an armed opponent). It doesn't matter if the opponent cuts directly at you, cuts in from the left or if an enemy cuts in from the right. If your mind becomes captive, even a little, to the enemy, his sword or to the moment itself the opponent will be able to read your movement and you will be cut.

Making conscious effort to understand the opponent's intent you will allow the enemy to see directly into your mind. If you allow your mind to be occupied by your movement, then your mind has been taken by your body. You cannot be conscious even of your own self. Thinking of your own mind and body is only something done by Shoshinsha (beginners).

Focusing your mind on your sword means that the sword has taken hold of your mind. Should you focus on the moment then the moment has taken hold of your mind. If you concentrate on your striking sword, then your mind has been taken by that. Concerning yourself with where your mind is and where it should best be focused, means that your mind has been taken by that action. With that you have become a husk, like the cast off skin of a snake or cicada. Those that train in the sword arts are aware of this.

Within Buddhism having the mind become prisoner to something is known as Mayoi, or being at a loss/going astray and is referred to as Mumyo Juchi Bonno Being Stopped by Polluting Thoughts Leads You Astray.

北斎漫画

Excerpt from:

Hokusai's Manga:

Jujutsu · Sumo · Torite Arresting Techniques

葛飾北斎
Katsushika Hokusai

1815

葛飾北斎　北斎漫画
Katsushika Hokusai
Hokusai's Manga

Jujutsu・Sumo・Torite Arresting Techniques

Self-portrait
1842 (age 82)

Katsushika Hokusai (1760 ~ 1849) began publishing volumes of his sketches starting in 1814. The 15 volume set *Hokusai's Manga* contains over 4,000 illustrations printed with light color. He began publishing them starting in 1814. This section will isolate the unarmed martial arts scenes which include Sumo, Jujutsu, Torite (Arresting Techniques) and joint locks.

Volume 1: Brawling

Volume 3: Sumo

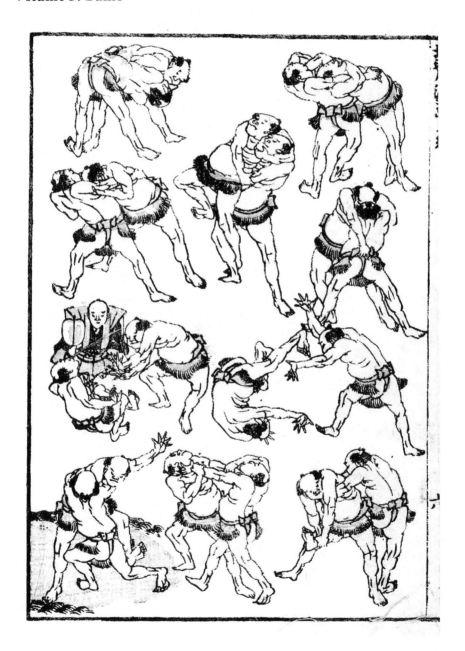

Volume 6: Torite Arresting Techniques, Ninjutsu & Joint Locks

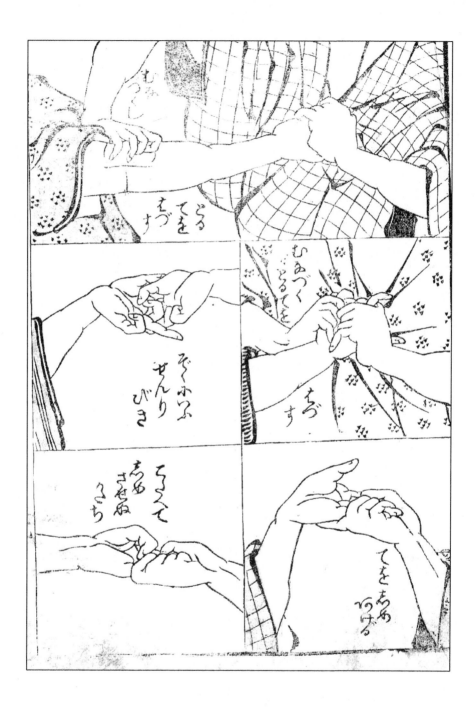

「むねづくし」「とるてをはずす」
If someone grabs your chest, this is how you remove the hand.

ぞくにいふ、せんりびき
（俗にいう千里引き）
This spot is called Senribiki, 1000 League Pull
Note: Senribiki refers to taking the fingers.

むねづく、とるてをはずす
If someone grabs your chest, remove it.

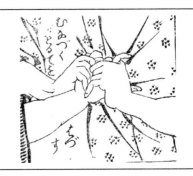

いたくて しめさせぬ かたち
Technique for causing an indescribable amount of pain.

てをしめあげる
Locking and raising the hand

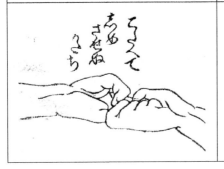

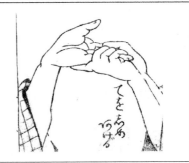

Volume 8: Skinny Guys Doing Sumo and Grappling

Volume 15: Solo Sumo Training

Volume 15: Children's Games

写真学筆
A Study in Truthful Painting 1815

The following works are by Maki Bokusen (1736-1824) a student and collaborator of Katsushika Hokusai. Bokusen worked with Hokusai on the publication of *Hokusai's Manga*.
The print dealer Richard Kruml states,

Bokusen and another of Hokusai's students, Tonansai Hokuun, are credited as copying Hokusai's drawings in preparation for the woodblock cutter as the term "ko" or "revisers" is used in the colophon, suggesting that it was the two pupils who arranged the varied sketches.

-Japaneseprints-london.com

Grabs, Joint-locks & Throws

Arresting Techniques:
Arresting Rope and Jutte (Police Truncheon)

Sumo and Feats of Strength

Note:
The rock is called a Chikara-Ishi, Rock of Strength, and weighs 39 Kan, 146 Kilograms / 321 pounds.

イデキシャリョウホウ

縊溺者療法

How to Treat Victims of Drowning or Hanging

by
澒原鐵二
Kahara Tetsuji

Police
Department
Library

1878

Idekisha Ryoho
Treating Victims of Drowning or Hanging

By Kahara Tetsuji 湏原鐵二
Police Department Library
January 4th Meiji 11 (1878)
Price 5 Sen

Eisha Ryoho
Resuscitating the Hanged
Illustration 1

縊者療法
第一圖

Eisha Ryoho
Resuscitating the Hanged Illustration 2

Resuscitating the Hanged (Explanation)
Chapter 1

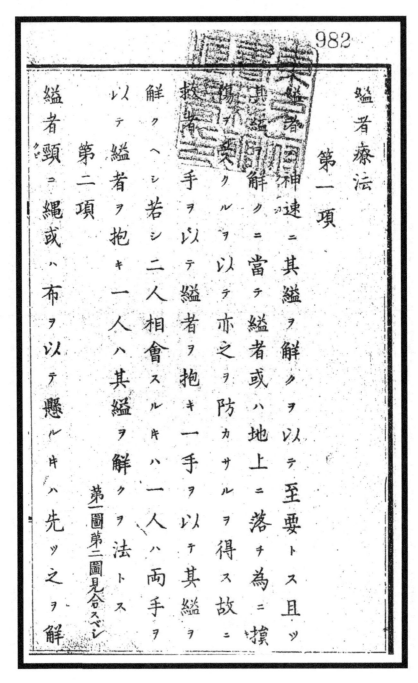

Treating Victims of Drowning or Hanging
By Kahara Tetsuji 湏原鐵二

Eisha Ryoho
Resuscitating the Hanged

Step 1

As soon as you discover a victim of hanging, it is extremely important that you swiftly remove whatever is around his neck. However, the victim can fall to the ground and further injure himself as you are untying or cutting that cord,. To prevent this, the rescuer should take some of the victim's weight with one arm and use the other arm to remove the noose. This is shown in Illustration 1.

If two rescuers are present, then one person can use both arms to lift the victim up while the other removes or cuts the noose. This is shown in Illustration 2.

Illustration 1	Illustration 2

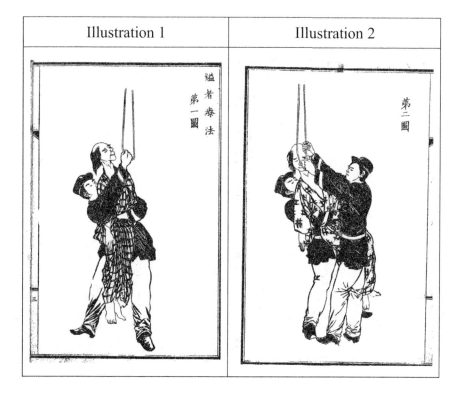

Resuscitating the Hanged (Explanation)
Chapter 2 & 3

第二項

縊者頸ニ縄或ハ布ヲ以テ懸ルヽ時ハ先ッ之ヲ解

キ放チ若シ其衣服ノ窄クシテ身ヲ繁繋セシ者

ナレハ亦皆之ヲ取除クヘシ

第三項

縊者ヲシテ外氣中或ハ空氣流通ノ室中ニ坐セ

シメ然後始メテ囘生ノ術ヲ施スヘシ且ツ其術

ヲ施スニ當テハ必用ノ人ノ外群集ヲ禁スヘシ

第一圖第二圖見合スベシ

Step 2

If you find a victim hanged with a rope or a piece of cloth (probably an Obi belt) then first remove that. Afterward, if he or she is wearing tight fitting clothing, this should be removed.

Step 3

The victim of hanging should be moved outside or seated in a room with good air circulation. Afterwards, you should begin Shisei no Jutsu, or resuscitation techniques. When performing this resuscitation ensure that any extraneous people are kept back.

Resuscitating the Hanged (Explanation)
Chapter 4

第四項

其術ヲ施スヤ鳩翎或ハ巻紙ヲ以テ鼻中及ヒ口

中ノ後部ヲ撫ッヘシ安母尼亜精藥アラハ之ヲ

鼻下ニ塗リ以テ其氣ヲ齅カシメ小腿及ヒ胸部

二八芥子泥ヲ貼付スヘシ若シ急ニシテ之ヲ供

スルニ時間ナキトキハ刷毛ヲ以テ摩シ且足

部ヲ摩擦シ之ヲシテ暖ナラシムヘシ 第三圖見
合スヘシ

Illustration 3

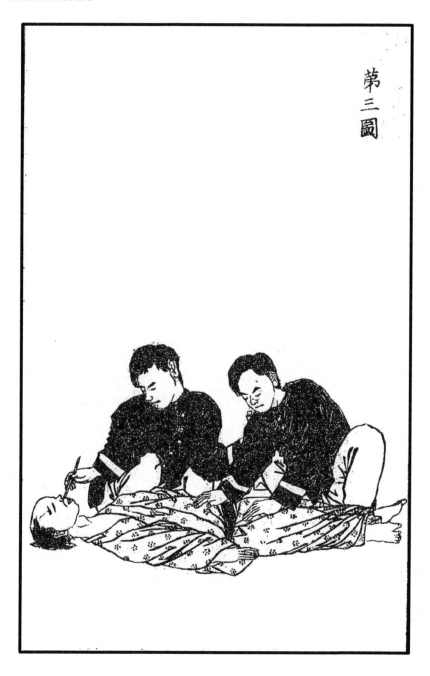

Step 4

To perform this technique first you will need a bird feather or a rolled up scrap of paper. Use the implement to penetrate deep into the nose and mouth of the victim. This will massage the back of the throat. This is shown in Illustration 3.

In addition, ammonia, such as the brand Araha, can be painted under the nose in order to stimulate the sense of smell. You can also make a paste of red pepper and spread it on pieces of paper. Then press these onto the chest and thighs of the victim.

If you are in a hurry or can't find a feather or paper, then a painting brush can be used to massage the soles of the feet. This vigorous rubbing and brushing of the feet will heat the victim up. Refer to illustration 3, below.

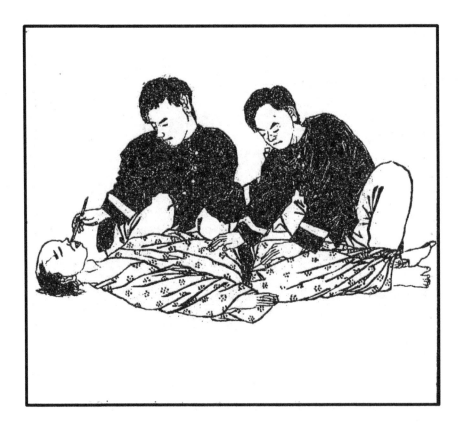

Resuscitating the Hanged (Explanation)
Steps 5, 6 & 7

第五項

醫負其塲ニ在テハ即チ刺絡ヲ行フヘシ

第六項

右之療法ヲ施シ尚呼吸セサル片ハ縊者ヲ左右
ニ動カシ而シテ其両手ヲ引キ擧ケ且其胃部ヲ
壓スル當ニ溺者ニ施ス所ノ如クスベシ蓋シ縊
者ニ於テモ亦此術ニ由テ空氣ヲ誘引スルヲ以

第七項

縊者生ニ復シ吸飲スルヲ得ハ少シク茶或ハ酒
ヲ飲マシムヘシ而メ之ヲ床ニ臥セ且頭ヲ高ク
シテ閒臥セシム

Illustration 4

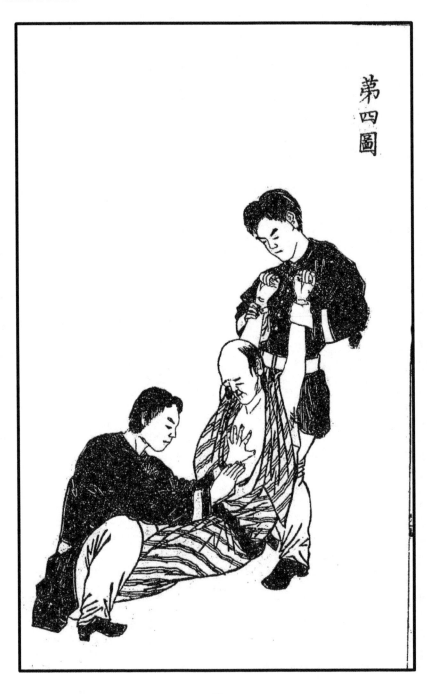

第四圖

Step 5

If the injury calls for it, bloodletting can be done on the spot.

Translator's Note: Some of the implements used for bloodletting in Japan. These are from *Useful Medical Implements: Volume 2* 医療筌蹄. 下巻 a Meiji Era Japanese translation of a book by Hermann Riedell.		
Scalpel	Blood Measuring Cup	Plate for Examining Blood
刀 葵 鋭 里	器 量 血	臣 于 磚 狀 皿

Step 6

If the rescuer has administered all the previous treatments and the patient is still not breathing, then the following should be done:

- Roll the victim back and forth, first onto his left side and then his right side. Next raise both his arms up.
- At the same time apply pressure to his stomach. This is the same technique that is applied to drowning victims. The purpose of this technique is to draw air into the body. This is shown in illustration 4.

Step 7

Once having recovered, a victim of hanging should be given something to drink. Give them some green tea or sake and then have the victim lay down and rest.

Dekisha Ryoho
How to Treat Victims of Drowning (Explanation)

溺者療法

溺者水中ヨリ取上ラレ未タ真ニ死相ヲ表ハサ

ルハ左ノ如ク所置スヘシ

第一項

口内及ヒ鼻孔ハ中指或ハ捲束セシ紙片ヲ以テ

カメテ之ヲ清潔ニスヘシ如何トナレハ溺者ノ

鼻孔口中ハ多ク泥石泡砂等ニテ呼吸ヲ障碍ス

ルコアレハナリ第一圖見合スヘシ

Dekisha Ryoho
How to Treat Victims of Drowning (Illustration 1)

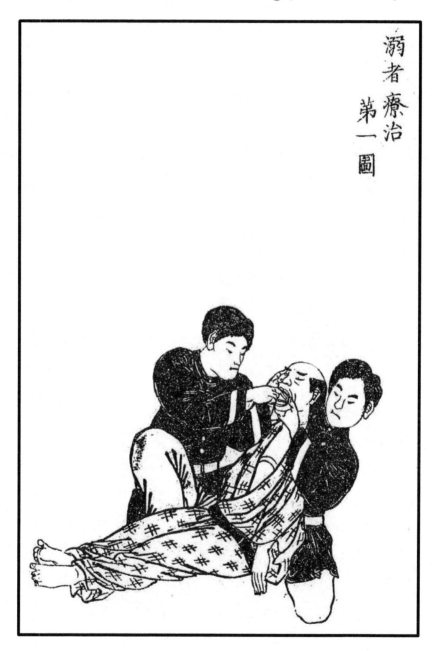

Dekisha Ryoho
How to Treat Victims of Drowning

Once a Oboremono, or drowning victim, has been recovered from the water, determine if there are any signs of life. If there are signs of life, follow the procedures written below.

Step 1

Use your middle finger or a piece of paper rolled into a tube and clean the inside of the victim's nose and mouth. No doubt there will be a lot of rocks, dirt, foam and sand in a drowned person's mouth and nose which prevent proper breathing. This procedure is shown in Illustration 1.

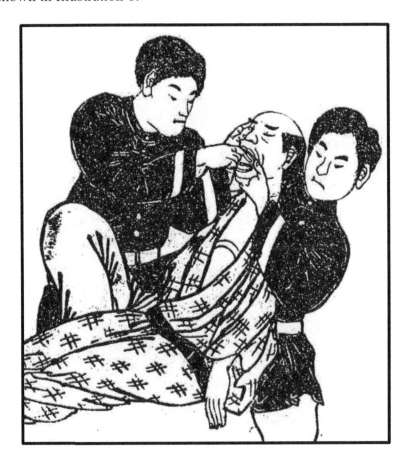

Step 2

You should lay the victim face down on the ground so that his head is slightly lower than his feet. His mouth and nose should be near the ground. Place a pillow under the victim's forehead. By doing this all the water that has been forced into his mouth and nose will be expelled.

If you have a plank of wood and raise the end under his feet, you can do all of the above quite easily. You will need to leave the drowning victim like this for 2 or 3 minutes. This is shown in Illustration 2, below.

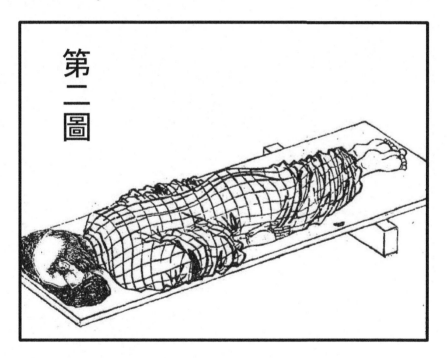

Step 3

Next, roll the drowning victim face up and raise his head. Transport him to a nearby house and then perform the procedures written below. However, if you judge that the situation calls for immediate action the following procedures should be done swiftly outside. This is shown in illustration 3, below.

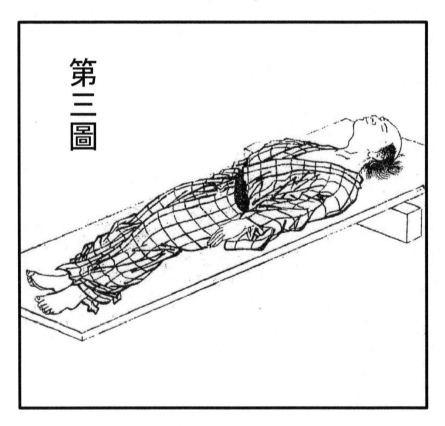

Step 4

You should immediately remove the drowning victim's wet clothing and rub his entire body down with a dry towel. If it is summertime then lay the victim out in the sunlight. However, don't let the sun shine directly on his face. This is shown in illustration 4, below.

Step 5

If there are two rescuers, then the second person can use a feather or rolled up piece of paper to clean out the back of the throat. After that, wipe down the chest and top of the head with cool water, then immediately rub vigorously with a dry cloth. See Illustration 5, below.

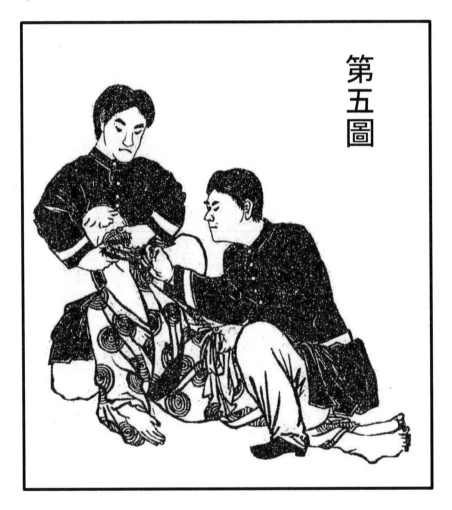

Illustration 6

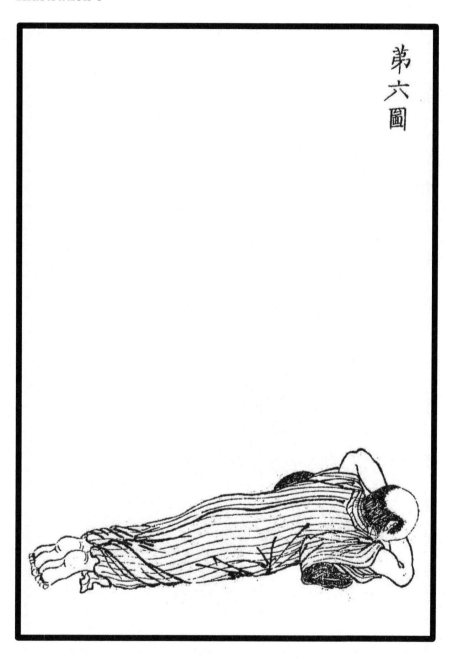

Illustration 7

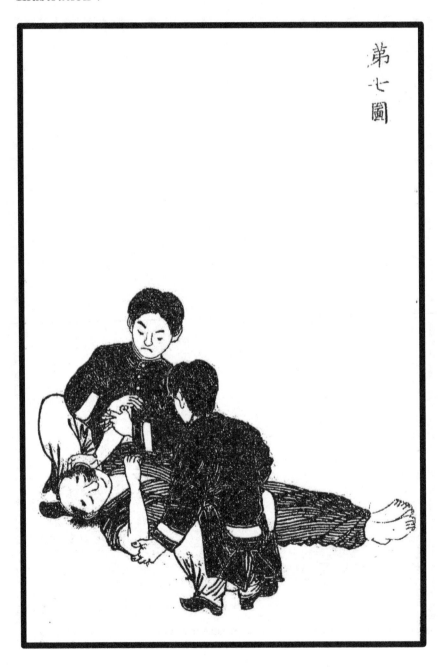

Illustration 8

Chapter 6

If the proceeding measures were not successful in restoring the victim's breathing, then try the following method:

First, roll the patient over, so he is face down. Ensure his head is positioned higher than his feet. Place a roll of cloth or clothing under his chest. Finally place the drowning victim's arms under his forehead to stabilize it.

The rescuers should take hold of the drowning victim's arms and torso and roll him over, then immediacy roll him face down. Over the course of one-minute roll the patient back and forth from his left side to his right side fifteen times. This procedure is shown in illustrations 6 ~ 8.

Illustration 6

Illustration 7   Illustration 8

Illustration 9

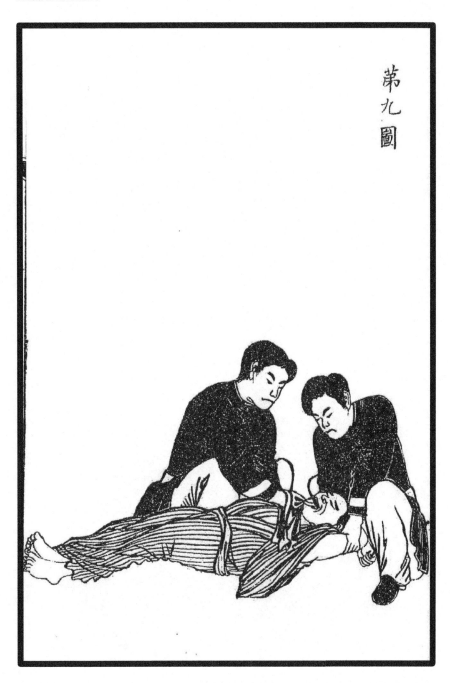

Illustration 10

第十圖

Chapter 7

If, after 2 or 3 minutes, breathing does not return then perform the following actions:

Roll the victim face up, placing whatever soft clothing or blankets are at hand to make a pillow and place it under his head. One of the rescuers should open the drowning victim's mouth and insert a finger deep into his mouth and pull out his tongue. Use a cloth or rag to firmly grip the end of the tongue. The other rescuer should take the drowning victim's arms and raise them above his head and then bring them down again against the victim's sides.

While one rescuer is manipulating the arms, the other rescuer should apply pressure. Applying pressure means pushing on the abdomen. This will force the internal organs up towards the chest. Release the pressure and then immediately push again. After releasing, the other rescuer, should immediately raise the victim's arms up and then push them down again to his sides, pushing in.

The purpose of the technique described above is to restore breathing. Over the course of one minute the rescuers should perform 10 repetitions. This method serves to restore breathing by expanding and contracting the chest. This procedure is shown in illustrations 9 &10.

Illustration 9   **Illustration 10**

第八項

溺者呼吸スルコヲ始ムレハ直チニ火ニテ煖メ

タル布ヲ以テ脚部及胃部ヲ温ムヘヒ而シテ其

吸飲スルヲ得ル者ニ在ツテ少レク茶或ハ酒ヲ

與フヘシ

第九項

其呼吸ヲ始メレ者再ヒ之ヲ閉止スルコト往々ア

リ然ルトキハ直チニ復タ其救助術ヲ施スヘシ

第十項

此救助術ハ溺者ノ呼吸ヲ發スル迄ニ施スヲ要

ス其溺者ノ身体蒼白寒冷シナ尽相ヲ現スルニ

非レトハ數時間ニ至ルモ決シテ救助術ヲ止ム可

ラズ

Chapter 8

When the patient begins breathing again, immediately light a fire nearby to help warm their body. Also wrap blankets around the patient's waist and legs to warm them. If the patient seems able to swallow have them drink some green tea or Sake.

Chapter 9

Patients that have recovered their breathing do sometimes stop breathing again. If this happens, restart the resuscitation techniques. It may, of course, be necessary to conduct resuscitation on individuals who are elderly or seem frail.

Chapter 10

Even if a drowning victim is elderly, or seems frail, the resuscitation methods described on the previous pages should be done. Such patients may appear pale and be cool to the touch, but if there is even the slightest sign of life, then you must continue to perform resuscitation for several hours.

第十一項

其救助術ヲ始行スルニ當リ直チニ醫師ニ報告スヘシ

第十二項

其救助術ハ窄小密閉ノ室ニ於テ施スヘカラス又多人ノ群集スルハ害アルヲ以テ其施術ニ關シ必用ノ人員ノミヲ現在セシムルヲ要ス

Chapter 11

Inform a doctor once resuscitation has begun on a patient.

Chapter 12

The resuscitation methods described in this book should not be conducted in a confined space with no air circulation. However, if onlookers gather around where you are treating the patient the crowd is liable to exacerbate the patients injuries, therefore unessential people should be kept back from the scene.

How to Treat Victims of Drowning or Hanging
By Kahara Tetsuji
澒原鐵二
Police Department Library
1878

End

兵法要務：
柔術剣棒図解秘訣

Excerpt from:

Fundamentals of
Military Strategy:
An Illustrated
Guide to the
Secrets of
Jujutsu, Kenjutsu
and Bojutsu

Part II
First Stage :
Standing Techniques

井口松之助
Inoguchi
Matsunosuke

1887

Translator's Introduction

This is continuing the introduction of Jujutsu techniques from the Tenjin Shinyo Ryu Jujutsu School. These Jujutsu techniques are from the *Fundamentals of Military Strategy: An Illustrated Guide to the Secrets of Jujutsu, Kenjutsu and Bojutsu.* It was written by Inoguchi Matsunosuke 井口松之助 and published in 1887. The Jujutsu in *Fundamentals of Military Strategy* contains five chapters:

1. 12 *Shikumi Tehodoki*, or Freeing Seized Hands Techniques.
2. 10 *Shodan Idori,* or First Level Responding to a Standing Attack techniques.
3. 10 *Shodan Tachi-ai,* or First Level Responding to Armed and Unarmed Attacks
4. 20 *Shodan Nagesute,* or First Level Sacrifice Throw techniques.
5. 20 Randori, Free Sparring techniques

The previous volume *A Collection of Curious Jujutsu Manuals Volume II* contained:

● 12 *Shikumi Tehodoki*, or Freeing Seized Hands Techniques.
● 10 *Shodan Idori,* or First Level Responding to a Standing Attack

This volume will contain a translation of the next section titled *First Stage : Standing Techniques : Ten Techniques.*

Shodan Tachiai Jutte 初段立合 十手

1. 行違 *Yuki Chigai* **Crossing Paths**
2. 突掛 *Tsuki Kake* **Attacked With a Punch**
3. 引落 *Hiki Otoshi* **Pulled Down**
4. 両胸捕 *Ryomune Dori* **Two Handed Chest Grab**
5. 連拍子 *Renhyoshi* **Joined in the Same Rhythm**
6. 友車 *Tomoguruma* **Roll Together**
7. 絹潜 *Kinu Katsugi* **Dropping and Loading Like Silk**
8. 襟投 *Eri Nage* **Collar Throw**
9. 手髪捕 *Tabusa Dori* **Someone Grabbing Your Hair**
10. 後捕 *Ushiro Dori* **Grabbed from Behind**

The author names the two combatants Koh, meaning former, and Otsu, meaning latter. To make the passages easier to understand, Koh will be "the Attacker" and Otsu will be "you."

Shodan Tachiai
Illustrated Guide to First Stage : Standing Attacks
行違 *Yuki Chigai* 1/10
Crossing Paths

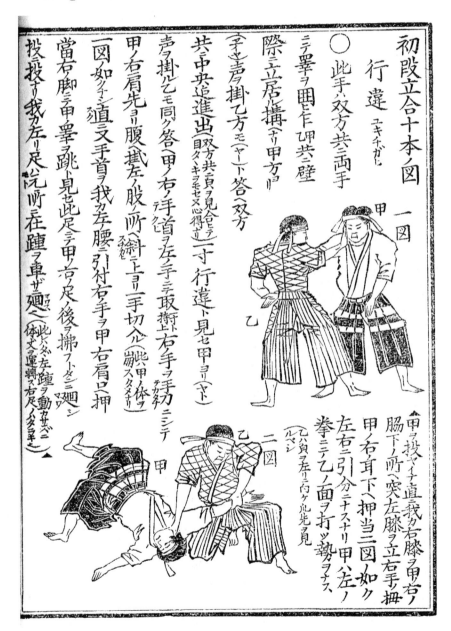

行違 *Yuki Chigai* Crossing Paths 1/10

This technique begins with both combatants standing on opposite sides of the Dojo next to the wall. You should both be standing in Kamae with your hands circling your groin.

The technique begins with the Attacker shouting a Kiai of *Ei-ya!* and advancing towards the center of the training area. You respond with an answering shout of *Yaa!* and move towards the center as well.

(Both combatants should fix their eyes on one another and remember that it is important not to blink.)[1]

The Attacker should make it appear he is going to pass by, when he suddenly shouts a Kake-goe of *Ya-toh!* You respond in the same manner and seize the Attacker's right wrist with your left hand. You should raise it up slightly as you strike the attackers neck where it meets his shoulder with your right hand in a Shuto, Knife-hand.

Then yank the Attacker's right arm diagonally downward towards your left thigh. (This will take your opponent's balance.) Then, as shown in Illustration 1, grip his right shoulder with your right hand and push down as you pull his right wrist to your hip.

Illustration 1

甲 一 図

甲 Koh
Attacker

乙 Otsu
You

---

[1] All information in brackets is by the author.

With your right foot, feint as if you are going to kick the Attacker in the groin, then use that leg to sweep his right leg. You are throwing him down with a Mawashi-Nage, Turning Throw.

When doing this throw, your left heel stays in place and you rotate on your left heel. (What this means is while your left heel stays in place, the rest of your body is rotating and following your right foot.)

Immediately after you throw the Attacker, plant your right knee by his right side while keeping your left knee up. Press the thumb of your right hand into the spot below his right ear.

Illustration 2

甲 Koh
Attacker

乙 Otsu
You

As shown in Illustration 2, you are pulling the Attacker to the left and right. Is right arm is being pulled to the left while you press into the spot below his right ear, forcing him to the right.

The Attacker will attempt to punch you in the face with his right hand. Avoid this by looking down at the toes of your left foot.

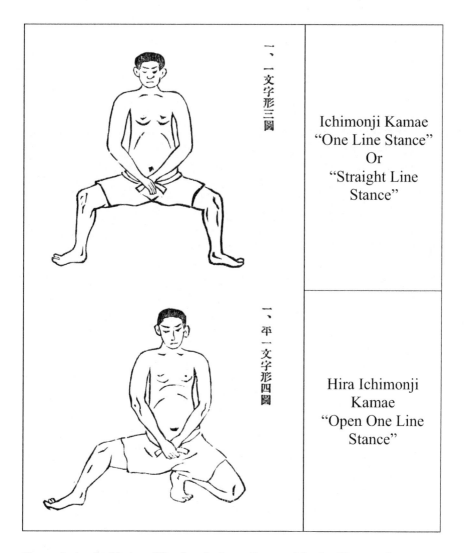

一、一文字形三圖	Ichimonji Kamae "One Line Stance" Or "Straight Line Stance"
一、平一文字形四圖	Hira Ichimonji Kamae "Open One Line Stance"

Translator's Note : The book doesn't specify the Kamae however the above two Kamae seem to be standard Kamae for this school. The images are from a different line of Tenjin Shinyo Ryu :

Illustrated Guide to the Inner Secrets of Tenjin School Jujutsu Kata: Hokoku Hall Tecchu School
By Kushi Niju 大串仁十
Published 1926

Shodan Tachiai First Stage : Standing Attacks 2/10
突掛 *Tsuki Kake*
Attacked With a Punch

七十五

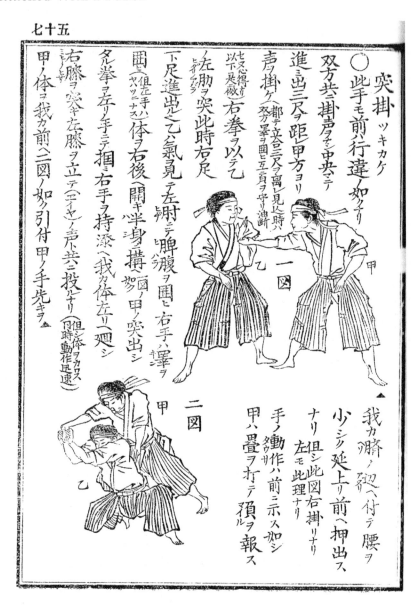

突掛 *Tsuki Kake 2/10*
Attacked With a Punch

This technique begins the same way as the previous one, Crossing Paths. You and the Attacker both shout a Kake-goe and advance towards the center of the training area. When the Attacker is about 3 Shaku, 90 centimeters, away he will shout a Kake-goe as he steps forward with his right foot and punches with his right fist. His target is Hidari Abara, or the ribs on your left side.

(Be sure to note that before the two combatants are 3 Shaku apart, both should have their hands circling their groin, ready to defend themselves. Each should be watching the other carefully.)

You have anticipated this strike a pull your left elbow in, covering your ribs and abdomen, while your right hand protects your groin. (However keep your left hand loose.)

Illustration 1

甲 Koh
Attacker

乙 Otsu
You

At the same time step back with your right foot and open up to the right. This means you have shifted your stance to Hanshi, or with your body perpendicular to the Attacker. This is shown in Illustration 1.

With your left hand seize the Attacker's right hand, the one he punched you with. Then grab with your right hand alongside your left. Rotate your body counter-clockwise and drop down onto your right knee, keeping your left knee up. Throw with a Kake-goe of *Eiya!*

(Remember that as you twist your body and drop down, you should increase your speed.)

Throw the Attacker in front of you.

Illustration 2

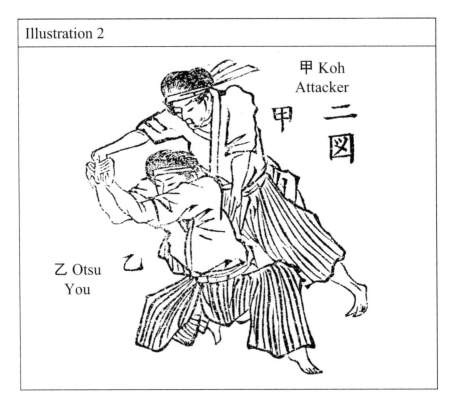

甲 Koh
Attacker

乙 Otsu
You

As Illustration 2 shows, when you are throwing, bring the Attacker's arms down to your navel. You should extend your back up and then forward as you throw.

(Note that these illustrations only show the right side, however the left side is done the same way.)

The Attacker attempts to punch you with his left hand the same way as in the previous technique. The opponent strikes the Tatami mats to signal his defeat.

Shodan Tachiai First Stage : Standing Attacks 3/10
引落 *Hiki Otoshi*
Pull and Drop

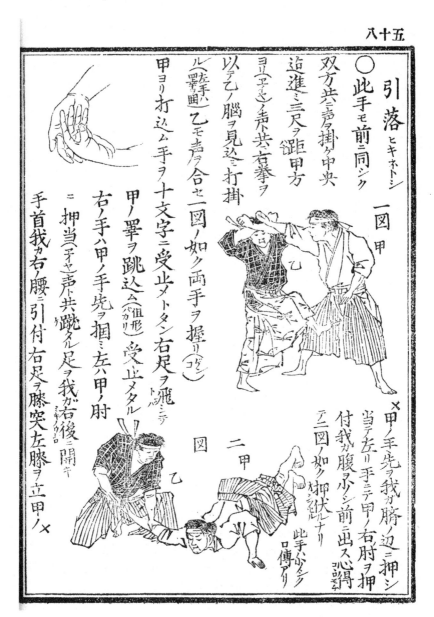

引落 *Hiki Otoshi* 3/10
Pull and Drop

This technique begins the same as the previous two. Both you and the Attacker shout a Kake-goe and advance towards the center of the training space. When you are about 3 Shaku, 90 centimeters, apart the Attacker shouts *Eiya!* and, at the same time, punches straight at your head with his right hand.
(Note that when punching, the Attacker keeps his left hand surrounding his groin.)
You match the Attacker's Kake-goe with your own and respond as shown in Illustration 1.

Illustration 1

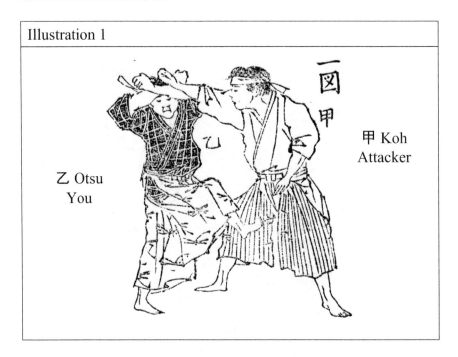

乙 Otsu
You

甲 Koh
Attacker

Squeeze both hands into fists.
(This is called Genko 拳固 "fist + hard.")
Block and stop the Attacker's strike with a Juji, cross-shaped block. Let your right foot fly up and kick the Attacker in the groin.
(Note that for training purposes this is *Katachi Bakari*, or just miming the action of kicking.)

Next, your right hand, which you used to block, should seize the Attacker's right wrist, while your left hand seizes his right elbow.

With a Kake-goe of *Eiya!* use the foot you kicked with to step back and to the right. As you do this, pull his wrist to your right hip. Keep your left knee up with your right knee on the ground. Keep the Attacker's wrist against your stomach near your navel. Your left hand should be pushing his right elbow down.

Illustration 2

乙 Otsu
You

甲 Koh
Attacker

Note that you should have your stomach pressed slightly forward. The Attacker should be brought down as shown in Illustration 2. There are a few minor Kuden about this technique.

Translator's Note: The text does not refer to the illustration with the hands but it seems to highlight the final hand position.

Shodan Tachiai First Stage : Standing Attacks 4/10
両胸捕 *Ryomune Dori*
Two Handed Chest Grab and Throw

九十五.

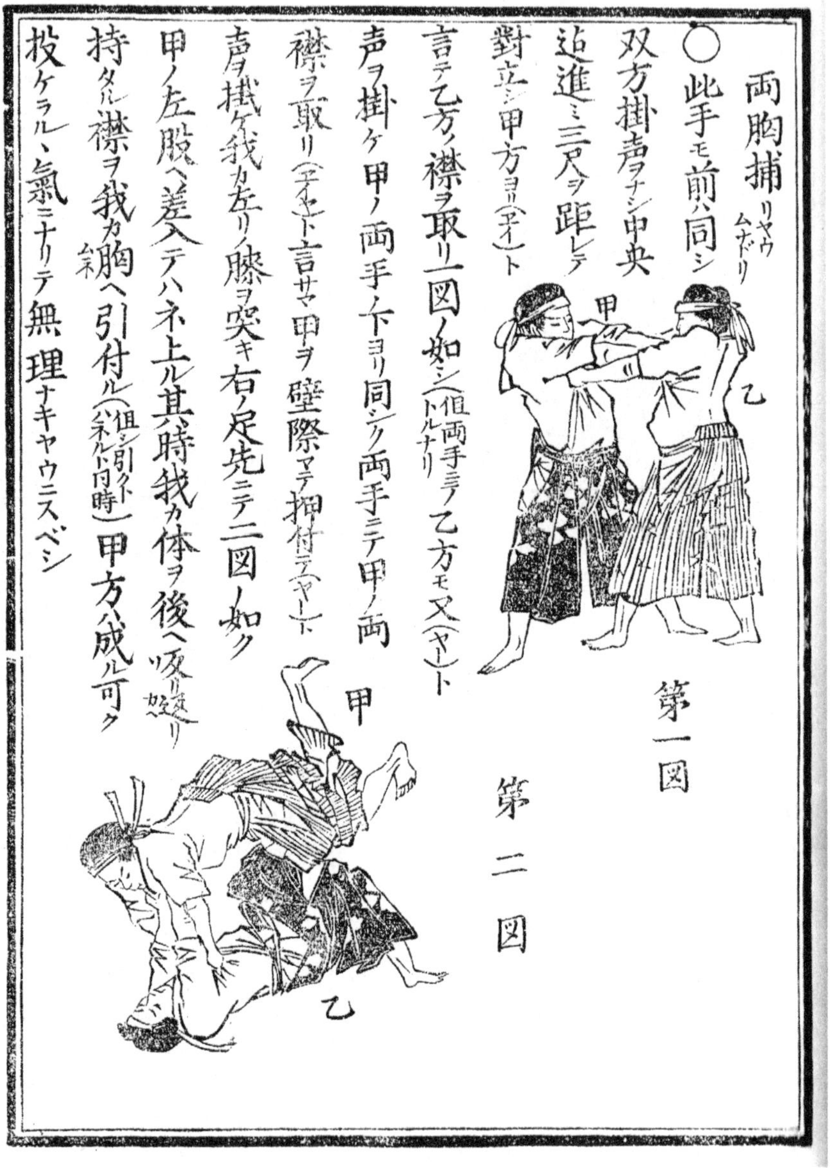

両胸捕
リヤウ
ム子ドリ

○此手モ前ハ同シ

双方掛声ナシ中央

迄進ミ三尺ヲ距レテ

對立シ甲方ヨリ（ヱイ）ト

言テ乙方ノ襟ヲ取リ一図ノ如シ（但両手ニテ乙方ヲ又（ヤ）ト

声ヲ掛ケ甲ノ両手ヲ下ヨリ同ジク両手ニテ甲ノ両

襟ヲ取リ（ヱイ）ト言サマ甲ヲ壁際マテ押付テヤリ（ト

声掛ケ我カ左リノ膝ヲ突キ右ノ足先ニテ二図ノ如ク

甲ノ左股ヘ差入テハネ上ル其時我カ体ヲ後ヘ（吸ヒ込ヒ）如ク

持タル襟ヲ我カ胸ヘ引付ル（但シ引ト（ネルト同時）甲方ハ成ル可ク

投ケラル、氣ニナリテ無理ナキャウニスベシ

甲

乙

第一図

第二図

乙

両胸捕 *Ryomune Dori* 4/10
Two Handed Chest Grab and Throw

This technique begins the same way as the previous one. Both you and the Attacker shout a Kake-goe and advance towards the center of the training area.

You both stop when you are about 3 Shaku, 90 centimeters, apart. With a shout of *Ei!* the attacker grabs your lapels as shown in Illustration 1.
(Note that this is a two-handed grab.)

Illustration 1	Illustration 2

You respond with a Ki-ai of *Yaa!* and reach below the Attacker's arms with both hands to seize his collar. Next, with a shout of *Eiya!* push the Attacker until he is against the far wall. After that, shout a Kake-goe of *Yaa!* and strike upward with your left knee. Slip your right leg forward until it is on the inside of the Attacker's left thigh.

After that, throw your body down and backwards so you roll over while holding onto the Attacker's lapels. Pull him towards your chest as you roll back.
(Note that you should be pulling and forcing him upwards at the same time.)

The Attacker will find himself being thrown. Practice this carefully so you can throw without effort.

Shodan Tachiai First Stage : Standing Attacks 5/10
連拍子 *Renhyoshi*
Joined in the Same Rhythm

十六

連拍子　ツレヒヤウシ

○此手ハ双方共ニ壁際ニ並立双方

畢ヲカコミ居リ甲方ヨリ（ヤ―ト声掛ケル

乙方モ之ニ應シテ共ニ中央マテ進

甲方ヨリ（エイヤト言サマ抱付カントスル乙モ

（ヤ―ト應シテ我ガ左リ手ヲ延シ甲ノ

左リ腰ニ手先ヲ掛ケ左リ足ヲ甲ノ右腿

ノ後ニ踏ミ張リ我ガ腰ヲ掛ク下ゲ図ノ

如クナシ（エイヤ）ト言サマ手ト腰トヲ捻ルトタシニ張タル

左足踏耐ヘテ手ヲ後へ捻倒スナリ

此図ハ左リ掛リナリ左右共同理ニシテ乙甲ノ左ニ在時ハ左リ連拍子右ハ右

連拍子ト号ス

乙

甲

連拍子 Renhyoshi 5/10
Joined in the Same Rhythm

This technique begins with both combatants standing against the wall on opposite sides of the training space. Both are standing with hands circling the groin.

The Attacker shouts a Kake-goe of Ya! and you respond with a shout of your own. You then both advance to the center of the training space.

The Attacker steps past you, shouts a Kake-goe of Eiya! and wraps his arms around you from behind. You respond with a shout of Ya! while extending your left arm and gripping his left hip. Then shift your left leg behind the Attacker's right thigh and drop your hips slightly. You should be positioned as shown in the illustration.

With a shout of Eiya! twist your arm and hips and put your weight on your left foot. As you twist you will topple your opponent over your leg.

This illustration only shows the technique on your left side. The principle applies to both the left and right sides. If the attacker is on your left side the technique is called Left Joined in the Same Rhythm. If it is done with the opponent on your right then it is called Right Joined in the Same Rhythm.

Shodan Tachiai First Stage : Standing Attacks 6/10
友車 *Tomo Guruma*
Roll Together

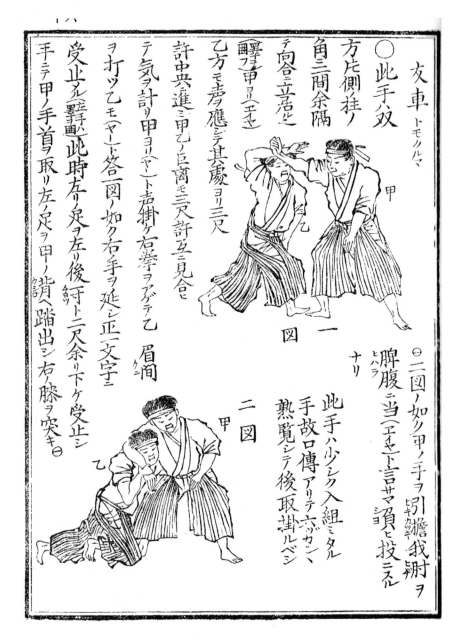

友車 *Tomo Guruma* 6/10
Roll Together

This technique begins with both combatants standing 2 Ken apart on opposite sides of the training space by one of the columns. The combatants should be facing each other.
(Note that the hands should be surrounding the groin.)

The Attacker shouts a Kake-goe of Eiya! and you respond with a shout of your own. You and the Attacker then advance 3 Shaku towards the center of the training area. When the distance between you and the Attacker closes to within 3 Shaku, you both lock eyes and judge each other's relative strengths and weaknesses.

With a Kake-goe of Yaa! the attacker raises his fist and punches to your Miken, the spot between your eyebrows. You shout Yaa! and respond as shown in Illustration 1. Raise your right arm up and block. Your arm is straight like Ichimonji, the Kanji for the number one, 一.
(Note that your left hand should be protecting your groin.)

Illustration 1

乙 Otsu
You

甲 Koh
Attacker

甲

図 一

103

At the same time, drop your left foot back and to the left about 2 Shaku, 60 centimeters. Using the arm you blocked with, grab the attackers right wrist. Then step behind the Attacker with your left foot while dropping onto your right knee.

As Illustration 2 shows, wrap the Attacker's right arm around your shoulders and strike him in Hibara, the side, with your left elbow. Shout a Kake-goe of *Eiya!* as you do this. Finally, do a Shoinage, load on the back and throw.

Since this technique involves getting in very close contact with your opponent there are Kuden, oral transmissions. Only train this difficult technique after you have studied the instructions carefully.

Illustration 2

甲 Koh
Attacker

乙 Otsu
You

Shodan Tachiai First Stage : Standing Attacks
絹潜 *Kinu Katsugi* 7/10
Dropping and Loading Like Silk

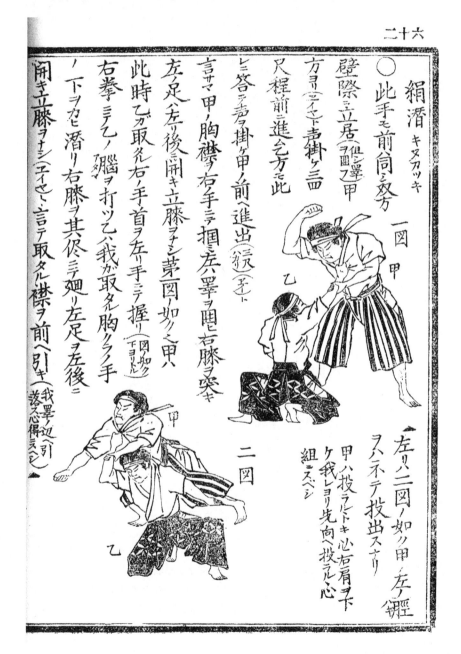

絹潜 *Kinu Katsugi 7/10*
Dropping and Loading Like Silk[2]

This technique begins the same way as the previous one. Both combatants are standing against the wall on opposite sides of the training area.

(Note that the hands are surrounding the groin, protecting it.)[3]

The Attacker shouts a Kake-goe of *Eiya!* and moves forward about 3 or 4 Shaku, 90 ~ 120 centimeters. You respond with a Kake-goe and move forward.

(Step forward about 90 centimeters.)

With a Kake-goe of *Ei!* seize the Attacker's left lapel with your right hand. Keep your left hand guarding your groin.

Next, plant your right knee on the ground and swing your left leg behind you. This is shown in Illustration 1.

Illustration 1

甲 Koh Attacker

図

甲

乙 Otsu You

乙

---

[2] The first Kanji means "silk" but the second Kanji means "to crawl or swim under something." The reading given for the second Kanji is Katsugi, which means "to load on the shoulder." I have included both meanings in the name of the technique.

[3] All the information in brackets is by the author.

Illustration 2

乙 Otsu
You

甲 Koh
Attacker

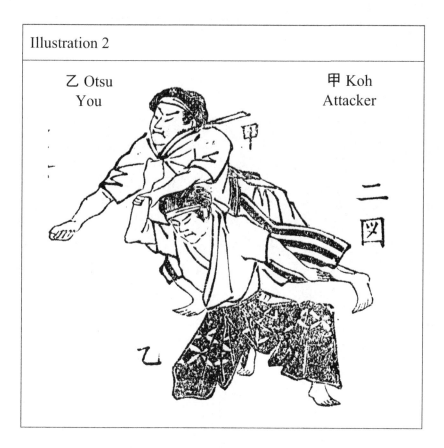

At this point the Attacker seizes your right wrist, which is holding his chest lapel with his left hand.
(As the illustration shows, he grabs your wrist from below.)

The Attacker then raises his right hand to strike you in the head. As he does this rotate counter-clockwise and back with your left foot. Keep your right knee on the ground and maintain your hold on his lapel with your right hand as you do this.

Then, with a Kake-goe of *Eiya!* pull his collar forward.
(Note that your goal is to pull him down in front of your groin.)

As Illustration 2 shows, push back on his shin with your left hand as you pull with your right. The shin is called *Hagi* or *Tsune* in Japanese. This will throw your opponent down in front of you.

Shodan Tachiai First Stage : Standing Attacks 8/10
襟投 Eri Nage
Collar Throw

三十六

襟投 エリナゲ
乙
甲

○双方前ノ如ク

畢ヲ囲ヒ乍壁際ニ立居之甲方ヨリ（アイト声掛ケ乙方モ答（テ）共ニ中央ヘ進ミ摺レ違フテ行スキセシ甲ノ後襟ヲ一圖ノ如ク取リ我ガ体ノ向キヲカヘエリヲ取タル手ノ下ヲ潜リ左膝ヲ突キ右ニ立（左手ハ）（ヤート声掛甲ノ襟ヲ我前ヘ引落ス（我ガ畢ノ）（辺ニ引ク）二圖如クナス甲ハ倒レナガラ直ニ右手ヲ（スデガヘシ）以テ乙ノ頁ヲ打×

一圖

二圖
甲
乙

×乙ハ投ルヤイナ甲我ガ面ヲ打ツ故ニ同シク手カヲ額ニ加ヘテ受止ルナリ

襟投 Eri Nage 8/10
Collar Throw

This technique begins the same as the previous ones, with both combatants standing against the wall on opposite sides of the training space. The hands should be protecting the groin.

The Attacker shouts a Kake-goe of *Ei!* and you answer with a shout of your own. Next, both of you advance towards the center of the training area. Just as you pass the Attacker, turn around and grab the back of his collar with your right hand. This is shown in Illustration 1.

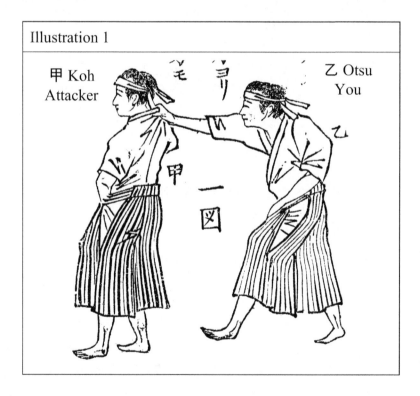

Illustration 1

甲 Koh
Attacker

乙 Otsu
You

You then turn so you are facing the opposite way. Drop down onto your left knee directly under the hand you grabbed his collar with. Keep your right leg upright.
(Note that your left hand should be protecting your groin.)

With a Kake-goe of *Yaa!* pull him down.
(Your goal is to make him drop in the area near your groin.)
This is shown in illustration 2.

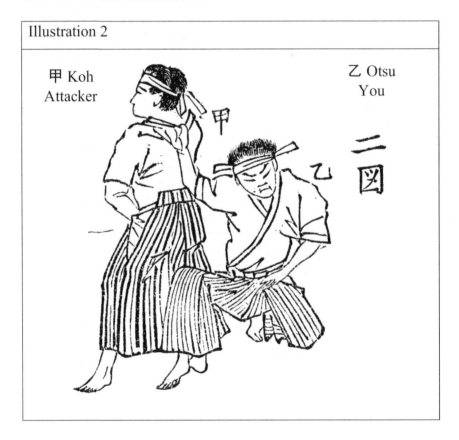

Illustration 2

甲 Koh
Attacker

乙 Otsu
You

As soon as the Attacker hits the ground he tries to punch you in the face with his right hand.
(This strike is a Shuto, knife hand.)

Since you are expecting this attack to your face, the moment you finish throwing you also make a Shuto and block the Attacker's strike to your forehead.

Shodan Tachiai First Stage : Standing Attacks 9/10
手髪捕 *Tabusa Dori*
Escaping From Someone Grabbing Your Hair

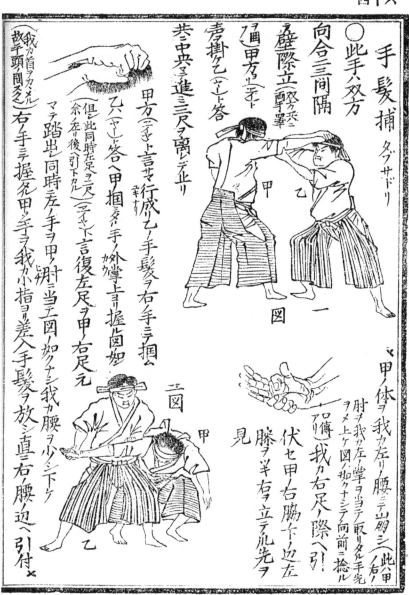

111

手髪捕 *Tabusa Dori* 9/10
Escaping From Someone Grabbing Your Hair

This technique begins with both you and the Attacker standing against the wall on opposite sides of the Dojo about 2 or 3 Ken, 3.6 ~ 5.4 meters, apart.
(The hands of both combatants should be protecting the groin.)

The Attacker shouts a Kakegoe of *Ei!* and you answer with *Ya!* You both advance towards the center and stop when you are about 3 Shaku apart.

The Attacker then shouts *Eiya!* and draws close grabbing your hair with his right hand. You respond with a shout of Yaa! and place your hand on top of his and grip. This is shown in the illustration.
(Note that at the same time you drop your left foot back about 2 Shaku, 60 centimeters.)

With a shout of *Eiya!* move your left foot again, stepping right beside the Attacker's right foot. At the same time, strike and grab the Attacker's right elbow with your left hand. You should be positioned as shown in illustration 1.

甲 Koh
Attacker

乙
Otsu
You

Next, drop your hips slightly.
(If you bend your head forward you will make a gap between the Attacker's hand and your head.)

You have seized the Attacker's right hand with your right hand. Start working the fingers of your right hand underneath the Attacker's hand, starting with your little finger. As soon as you free your hair, break his balance by pulling his right arm down beside your right hip forcing the Attacker's body beside your left hip.
(You are able to do this since you have the Attacker's elbow in the palm of your left hand and the end of his right hand in your right hand. This is shown in the illustration. You are twisting him forward. There is a Kuden, oral transmission, regarding this point.)

Pull the Attacker down beside your right foot. Plant your left knee in his right side, below his armpit, while keeping your right knee upright. Keep your eyes focused on the tips of your toes.

This combines the illustrations from this book along with the ones in *Illustrated Guide to the Inner Secrets of Tenjin School* by Kushi Niju 大串仁十, published in 1926. The title of the technique is the same but there are some variations since this is from a different line of Tenjin Shinyo Ryu .

1	2

3	4

Shodan Tachiai First Stage : Standing Attacks
後捕 *Ushiro Dori* 10/10
Grabbed From Behind

五十六

後捕 （ウシロドリ）

○此手ハ前ノ居捕ノ後取ノ通リナリ

只立合ノ仕組ナリ乙方壁際ヨリ四尺

斗リ隔テ両手ニ拳テ囲ヒテ立ツ甲方其

後ヨリ（エイセ）ト声掛ケ乙ノ背ヨリ抱ク

第一図ノ如クナリ乙モ（ヤ—ト答テ前

ノ如ク我ガ背頭額ヲ甲ノ顔ヘ（左ノ顔ヲ
右ノ顔ヘ付ル）

一寸当直ニ我ガ両肘ヲ張ル（此伸ヲ
抱ル）

両手ヲスカシ
（伸ヲ抜ルヲ多）前ノ居捕ノ如キ手ニテ躰ヲ下ゲ

右ノ膝ヲ突キ左足左ノ後ニ開キ（ヱイサ）ト言サマ

甲ヲ前ヘ引キ投ルナリ甲ハ投ラルト片乙ノ向ヘ

已ヨリ先ヘタヘル心ニテ我額ガ乙ノ臍ニ当ル位ニ心得ベシ

後捕 Ushiro Dori 10/10
Grabbed From Behind

This technique is the same as the earlier technique from Idori, Seated Techniques, which is also called Ushiro Dori. However, since this section is Tachi Ai, Standing Techniques, it is done while standing. Other than that, it is done the same as the earlier technique. You begin this technique standing near a wall with your hands surrounding your groin. The Attacker stands about 4 Shaku, 120 centimeters, behind you. He shouts a Kakegoe of Eiya! and then begins approaching you from behind. When he reaches you, he wraps both arms around you from behind. This is shown inn Illustration 1.

乙
Otsu
You

甲 Koh
Attacker

You shout *Ya!* and respond as you did in the Ushiro Dori in the Seated Techniques. Swing your head back so you hit the Attacker in the face.

(The Attacker should turn his head to the left to avoid getting hit with the back of your head.)

At the same time, push your elbows out to the sides.

(This will enable you to escape his arms.)

Then use your hands in the same way as described in the Seated Technique version of this technique. Drop down and plant your right knee on the ground and pull your left foot back. With a shout of *Eiya!* pull the Attacker and thrown him forward.

The Attacker should be prepared to be thrown forward over his opponent. The Attacker should end up with his forehead near his opponent's navel.

Translator's Note: This is the seated version of Ushiro Dori from the Shodan: First Level.

In this technique you are seated in Seiza, approximately 3 Shaku, 90 centimeters, away from the wall with your arms held wide and ready. Your hands are encircling your groin.

The opponent, who is seated behind you, shouts a Kake-goe of *Eiya!* Before pressing his right knee into the ground and standing up on his left foot and grabbing you from behind. This is shown in illustration 1.

You respond with a shout of *Yaa!* and whip your head back to strike the Attacker's forehead. The person in the role of the Attacker should turn his head to the left to avoid being struck during training. Next, extend your body upward slightly by putting your weight on your right knee as you swing your left foot out to the left as you stand on it.

With a Kake-goe of *Yaa!* expand your elbows out in order to force off the Attacker's grip. As soon as you do this, grab the Attacker's shirt on his right shoulder with your right hand and push on the shin of his left foot with your left hand. With a Kake-goe of *Eiya!* pull down hard with your right hand, drop your hips down and throw the Attacker. This is shown in illustration 2.

After you finish the technique you should immediately return to a ready position, with your hands surrounding your groin and watching the Attacker for any signs of a counterattack.

During training the Attacker should be careful not to land hard on his right shoulder. You should be careful to throw the Attacker lightly.

The Fundamentals of Jujutsu

A Study in Physical and
Psychological Development
Volume 1

By Yamada Kajiro
山田嘉十郎

1909

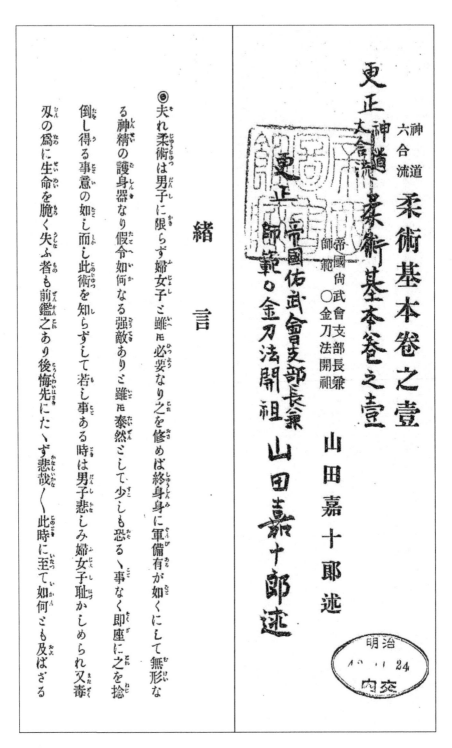

神道 六合流 柔術基本巻之壹

更正大合流 柔術基本巻之壹

帝國尚武會支部長兼 ○金刀法開祖

更正神道

師範 帝國尚武會支部長兼 ○金刀法開祖 山田嘉十郎述

更正師範 ○金刀法開祖 山田嘉十郎述

明治
24
内交

緒　言

◉夫れ柔術は男子に限らず婦女子と雖圧必要なり之を修めば終身に軍備有が如くにして無形なる神精の護身器なり假令如何なる強敵ありと雖圧泰然こして少しも恐る〻事なく即座に之を捻倒し得る事意の如し而し此術を知らずして若し事ある時は男子悲しみ婦女子恥かしめられ又毒双の爲に生命を脆く失ふ者も前鑑之あり後悔先にたゝず悲哉〱此時に至て如何こも及ばざる

122

The Fundamentals of Jujutsu from the Shinto Taiki School Volume 1

By Yamada Kajiro
Imperial Ubu Society Branch Chief
Head Instructor
Founder of the Golden Sword Method[4]

Introduction

Jujutsu is not exclusively for men, it is also an art that women and girls should train. If you become adept at Jujutsu your entire body, from the top of your head to the bottom of your feet, will be like an army ready to fight. Further, the shapeless and indescribable state of mental readiness that develops in tandem with Jujutsu training will be your weapon.

For example, no matter how strong an opponent may be, you will be able to confront them easily and without the slightest trace of fear. You will feel confident you can stop any attack and topple any foe. However, being ignorant of the art of Jujutsu will result in the sadness of defeat for men and the shame of being abused by women. There are countless sad examples throughout history of people being cut down by an assassin's poisoned dagger and the anguish felt by those left behind.

So, to prevent such an unfortunate series of events I feel it is essential that I present a quick introduction to Jujutsu.

---

[4] Note: The handwritten notes at the top of the page are corrections to some of the Kanji that were incorrectly printed. The Kanji 六 was mistakenly used instead of 大 and 尚 mistakenly used instead of 佑 I was unable to locate a "Volume 2."

Cautions

なり今茲に因て之を思はば速に此術を學ばずんばあるべからざる事なり

◉特に注意す可き事

◉偖柔術は護身の爲に學ぶべき術にして非常の外は假令遊戯にもせよ使用すべからず又他見他言

をもなすべからず又之を猥りにせば大害ごなる能々注意し且愼むべき事なり

◉柔術には極意ご云ふ秘して公言せざる術あり此術は至極深意斯道上愼重且つ猥りに行はざるの

意味にして危急存亡に關する時に至り初めて止を得ざる塲合に用ゆる術なり又極意にも金刀法

ご云ふ術あり此法は我が發明に係る古今未曾有の奇術なり此術は實に神速且つ偉大なる強剛術

なりご云ふべし是皆深く愼み注意肝要なる事なり

◉此書を讀み自修せんご欲せば唯讀過する而已にては其効鮮なし先づ敵手を求め使手ごなり又受

手ごなり其情實を考究し猶幾回ごなく習熟し十分意に達する迄數重ねて試むべし而せば自然自

得する事なり然れモ廣く熟練し且つ上達せんご欲せば各地此術を得たる師に就き實地學ばる丶

Cautions

1. The purpose of learning Jujutsu is self-defense and it shouldn't be employed except in case of emergency. For example, the Jujutsu arts should never be used in a tournament where gambling is being done. In addition, it is not something you should show or talk about with other people. If you use Jujutsu in a shameful way, disaster will surely befall you. You should be extremely careful regarding the above points and take them to heart.

2. Within Jujutsu there are a set of techniques known as Gokui Jutsu, Inner Mysteries Techniques. These techniques are never discussed openly in public and they are cherished due to the profound underlying meaning attached to them. In addition, no insincere actions may be taken to sully that purity. These techniques are only used in a life or death situation and as a matter of last resort. Within the Gokui there is a technique known as the Golden Sword Method which was developed by me. This wondrous technique has no parallel now or in the past. This magnificently powerful technique can be employed with divine swiftness. I would very much like for everyone to pay close attention to, and appreciate the fundamental aspect of, this technique.

3. If you were to simply read this document without intending to practice the lessons held within, the benefits of this book will be meager. The first step is to find a training partner and take on the role of the Tsukai-te, the one performing the techniques. After that, switch to the role of Uke, the one having the technique done on him. Having done both roles, consider how the training went and its effects. Repeat this process several times and train until you have thoroughly absorbed the movement and meaning of the techniques. By layering practice atop practice, you will naturally develop competency. This will greatly improve your fitness and ability. If you seek to master these techniques, then inquire with one of the master instructors in your region and you will be able to learn directly from them. Ideally, a reader would apply to learn at my Dojo. By joining the Dojo and learning directly from me, you will receive direct transmission of Jujutsu techniques. My fast learning system will allow anyone to make rapid progress.

Illustration 1

も可なれゞも最も又我が道場にて實習希望の方は入會あれば諸術ゞも直接實地に速成教授する

者なり

◉ 第壹條

抑々柔術には種々の流名あれゞも執る處當る處終始一貫少しも違ふ事なく今茲に圖せるは稽古着並びに身搆への大意なり夫れ右なる白き襦袢に猿股引を着たるは使手なり黑き襦袢に猿股引を着たるは受手なり又此圖は受手使手對面に座して禮式を致し此禮式は一間を隔て、禮するを正式とす既に禮終つて心ろ靜かに身を搆へ徐々にして互に近より互に進み隱顯虚實互に相見合相互に油斷なく又眼光は尖ごく氣力神正よして動作も又活潑なり且其勇は高尙何れも偉大なる深意を含み乍ら互に對峙し互に力を込め兩手を兩膝の上部に置又全身には少しも

Chapter 1: How to Begin

Even though there are many different schools of Jujutsu, they all grab, strike, begin training and end training in the same way. The illustration shows an overview of Jujutsu practitioners facing off against each other wearing Keikogi, or training uniforms.

The person on the right in the white Juban shirt and Saru Matabiki "Monkey Pants" is the Tsukaite, the person applying the technique. On the left in the black Juban shirt and Saru Matabiki "Monkey Pants" is the Ukete, the person receiving the technique.[5]

This illustration shows both combatants kneeling facing each other in the ceremonial display of respect. The official way to begin this ceremony of respect is to start one interval (180 cm) apart. The combatants bow to each other. Having completed the bow, both combatants first calm themselves before advancing slowly toward the other, shrinking the distance between them.

Both Jujutsu practitioners are using *Inken Kyojitsu*, which means trying various strategies to judge how the opponent reacts while concealing their own intentions. They are observing each other and ascertaining the other's ability without becoming careless. Their eyes are sharp, glittering with the intensity of their martial spirit. Their movements are fluid as they both ready themselves to commit fully.

The martial bravery they display is dignified and reflective of how fully the inner meaning of Jujutsu training has permeated their being. With that feeling the two face off against each other, bringing their power to bear. Though their hands are placed just above the knees neither reveals any weaknesses in their defenses. Both are relaxed as they gradually close the distance, however they remain ever vigilant. When the interval decreases from 180 cm to around 30 cm the moment of truth has at last come. Both are ready for the match to begin. It is important that all the points discussed in this outline of *How to Begin* are followed accordingly.

---

[55] For clarity the person performing the technique will be "You" and the other person "the Defender."

Illustration 2

隙なく愈々迫り愈々警戒して双方の間だ六尺より譏か一尺前後ミ相成り誠に危機一發にして今に

も捕初めんミする處なり先身搆は大畧斯の如く爲さずんばある可からざるなり

◎第貳條

總て人ミ取組ミする時は圖の如く

立合なり受手は先づ右の手を延ば

し使手の胸襟又は肩襟を摑み左の

手で使手の右の袖下即ち八口の處

を摑み使手も又受手ミ同樣相互に

摑み合双方其心持油斷なく防ぎ合

ふものなり又使手茲に愈々受手を

右へ倒さんミせば使手は受手の躰を右へ引我が足も又右へ引又受手を左へ倒さんミせば使手は受

手の躰を左へ引我が足も又左へ引常に腰を屈めざる樣注意すべし然し受手を投るには先づ左の手

Chapter Two: Sharp Tug

You should train as shown in the illustration. The Defender reaches out with his right hand and grabs your Mune-eri, collar at the chest, or Kata-eri, collar at the shoulder. His left hand should grab the Sode-shita, or bottom of the sleeve. The "bottom of the sleeve" is also known as Yatsu-Guchi, or Eight Mouths. It is the open slit under the armpit on Japanese upper Kimono. You take hold of the Defender in the same manner, so you are both gripping each other in the same way.

Now you both begin defensive strategies, never letting your guard down. Seeing a chance present itself, you decide to topple the Defender to the right. To do this, pull the Defender's body to the right while stepping out with your right foot. If you want to topple the Defender to the left, then pull left and step to your left. When in the role of the attacker, make sure to always keep your back straight.

To actually throw the opponent you need to do a Hiki-Zuke, sharp tug, with your left hand to draw the Defender's attention before doing a Kuzushi, or balance breaking action, with your right hand. You can also alternate between pushing and pulling in order to bring the defender's center of gravity below your waist.

The moment you distract the Defender with a Hiki-Zuke, attack the ankle, shin or the side of the knee.[6] Use your heel or the arch of your foot to strike. In order to topple the Defender your attack can be a sweep, a hook or an upward scooping motion.

---

[6] Terminology used in this section:
Ankle: *Kuro-fushi* "Black Joint"
Knee: *Hiza*
Shin: *Tsune*
Heel: *Kakato/ Kubisu*
Arch of the Foot: *Tsuchi Fumazu* "Never Touches the Ground"

Illustration 3

Chapter 3: Revolving Toss

This technique begins the same way as the previous one. You and the Defender are gripping each other's chest and the slit at the armpit. You should push and pull on the Defender and try a variety of close-range strategies. If, at one point, the Defender leans forward, then you should not overlook this chance. Fall backwards and throw the Defender overhead. Do this by allowing your left foot and lower back to strike the ground as you pull with both hands.

Plant your right foot on the Defender's thigh, belt or just below the navel. With your right hand gripping the Defender's chest and your left hand gripping the slit under the armpit, pull hard as you can. Using a kicking motion with your right foot roll back and throw. This is called Hane Kaeshi, throw over. The Defender will end up on his back. You should recover and hold the Defender down.

Illustration 4

既に前に述たる第二條第三條の捕方と同じく先づ其虚實を見計り素早きを専一とす此圖の如く使

手受手相互に胸襟さ掴み合揉合内受手の隙を見て受手の右の脇下へ潜り込み同時に受手

の右の腕を我が右の肩へ擔き此時

受手の右の手は我が左の手で執り

右の手で受手の肩襟を掴み前へ屈

むと同時に受手の手を下へ引張り

乍ら我が右の足は前へ出し左の足

は後ろさし踏張り腰を入れ躰へ力

らを極めて脊負て前へ投付るなり

第

四

條

132

Chapter 4: Shoulder Throw

This technique begins the same way as the 2nd and 3rd techniques. The strategy for this technique is to start off with a series of misleading attacks and wait for the perfect moment. When you see an opening you rapidly execute this technique. As the illustration shows, both you and the Defender are gripping each other at the chest and armpit. You are engaged in a push-and-pull struggle known as Momi-ai in Japanese.

When you see an opening, sink down and move under the Defender's right armpit while, at the same time, loading the Defender's right arm on your right shoulder. Take hold of the Defender's right wrist with your left hand. Grip his right shoulder with your right hand. Next, bend forward and step forward with your right foot and, at the same time, pull the Defender's arm down. Your left foot should be planted firmly behind you. Put all your power in your hips, as you load up the Defender and throw.

Illustration 5

◎第五條

此捕方は第一條の如く正式の禮絡つて受手使手對座して第一圖の如く受手は

右の手にて使手の胸襟を片手で執なり

此時使手は氣をしづめ手つき神速に右

の手にて腕襟を摑み居る受手の手首を握り叉

左の手にて同じく受手の二の腕を握り握り乍ら

兩腕に力を入れて開つさ掛聲して其胸

にある受手の手を眼前へ衝出し外し外すや

第五條第一圖

134

Illustration 5.1

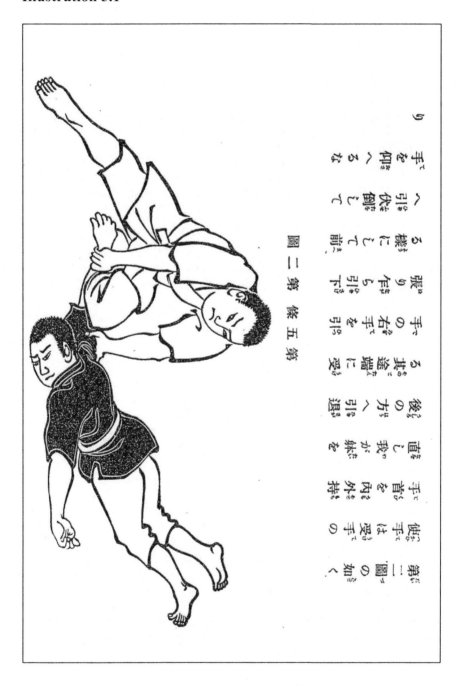

第二條五第

り手を引く様に腰手で其後、直を手で做方
を仰伏せにしの右手で首をは二圖の
引く引く方我が首を受手の
な下、に引へ肉を受手で如
る前、引下、退を外手の
で引、受け、持て、知くく

Chapter 5: Seated Arm Throw

This technique begins after the bowing in ceremony shown in Chapter 1. You and the Defender are facing each other. As shown in Illustration 1 (left,) the Defender reaches out with his right hand and grabs your chest lapel. You should remain calm and focused. Suddenly, with nearly divine speed, you use your right hand to grab the Defender's right wrist, which is holding your chest lapel. With your left hand grab the Defender's Ni no Ude, or bicep. Focus your power in your arms and, with a Kagegoe of *Ya!*[7] shove the Defender's right arm off your chest and straight at the Defender's eyes.

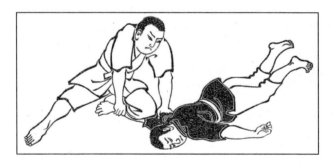

As Illustration 5.1 (above) shows, you switched your grip on the outside of the Defender's bicep from palm down to palm up. As you pull your body back, yank the Defender's arm and push it down. This will cause the Defender to fall flat in front of you. Finally, suppress the arm.[8]

---

[7] The Kakegoe is a shout that unifies the mind's intent with the body's action. The Kanji used means "open." This Kanji is not read as *Ya!* but this school uses it this way.

[8] The author's explanation is very brief. It appears you shift your whole body to your right as you push his arm down.

Illustration 6

◎第六條

此捕方は第五條さ同じく對座して捕り初めたるなり第一圖の如く

受手より兩手にて使手の胸襟を兩手で執り堅く摑みたる處なり此時

使手は先づ胸を張り張るや同時に兩手を受手の兩手の間だへ上より下へ押へ挿入れ嚴しく兩肱を張り左右へ排

第六條第一圖

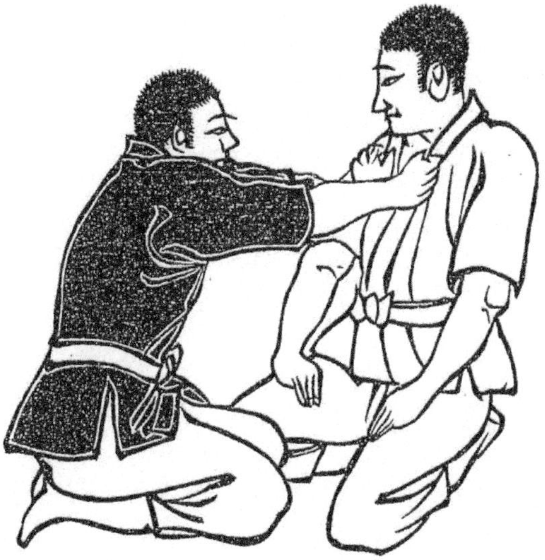

137

Illustration 6.1

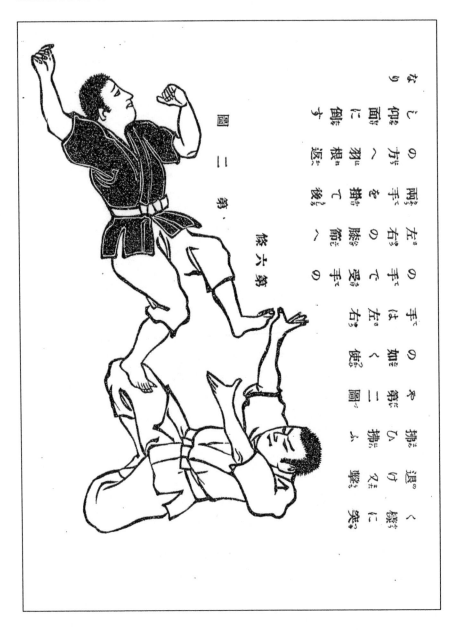

第六條

第一圖

なり仰向方へ面が掛の膝に羽根手で御錠と後しく返す

左の手の右の手は始め第に飛び退く膝にを膝の受が右使ふ圖ム撃突

Chapter 6: Seated Throw Back

This Torikata starts off the same way as Chapter 5 with both combatants facing each other, while seated in Seiza. As Illustration 6 (left) shows the Defender reaches out with both hands and grabs your front chest lapels and grips tightly.

First, push out your chest, then, at the same time strike upward with your arms, using ferocious strength. Your aim is to thrust your arms between the Defender's outstretched arms and use your elbows to knock his arms aside. After striking the arms and sweeping them aside, you should then do what is shown in Illustration 6.1 (below.)

Slip your left and right hands under the Defender's knees and flip him backwards in a Hane Gaeshi. The Kanji used for Hane Gaeshi mean "to throw at the point the wings join the back of a bird." This will cause the Defender to land flat on his back.

Illustration 7

◎第七條

此投方は第一圖の如く受手は右の方に座し使手は左の方に座し互に竝び座したる處なり偖此時受手より使手の胸襟を横斜面に左の手で執りたるなり使手は隙さず先づ右の手で受手の衣紋の處へ手を打掛け摑み又左りの手は受手の臍の處即ち前の帶を執り同時に使手は受手の眼前即

第七條第一圖

140

Illustration 7.1

第七條二圖

りあらちを入゛の瞬ゞにら
て割と面を抱だれ手での如にて臨べ膝な
抑るに曲てに如く筋つ下を
面どに接してく即くに撮ゝ横
に後ろ力左はゝと
投與右圖
付け回手同の
るなせにを横と

Chapter 7

This throw begins from the position shown in Illustration 7 (left.) The Defender sits to your right and you are to his left. You are both sitting beside each other in Seiza.

The Defender reaches across with his left and grabs your chest lapel. You, without a moment's hesitation strike to Eh-mon, the point where the Juban shirt crosses the chest.

After striking Eh-mon, grab the shirt there. With your left-hand grab near the Defender's navel. In other words, the front of the Obi, or belt. The second you grab the Obi, drop down in front of the Defender and roll as you land in front of his knees.

As shown in the Illustration 7.2 (above,) put strength in your left and right arms and use your falling weight to do a Kyoku Nage, bending throw. In other words, you are holding on to the opponent as you roll diagonally across your back, causing the Defender to land on his back, face up.

Illustration 8

◉第八條

此捕方は受手より兩手にて圖の如く使手の兩手首を執りたるなり

此時使手は我が兩手を引外さんさして先づ左の手を動かし試る受手は其の動く手を猶を堅く握るを使手は其を油斷を計り素早く右の手を引外し又左の手も引外すや否哉使手は右の手にて受手の胸を平手で衝突け左の手にて受手の膝節を横挑ひして仰面に倒し倒すや手を執るなり

第八條

143

Chapter 8

This Torikata begins with the Defender grabbing your wrists as shown in the illustration above. The natural response to this will be to pull your hands away. First, you try to pull back your left hand. The Defender will respond by gripping that wrist tighter. You should make use of that misdirection and rapidly yank your right hand free and then pull your left hand free.

As soon as you have done this, strike the Defender's chest with your right palm as you sweep his right knee with your left hand. This will topple the Defender onto his back. This is the end of the techniques.

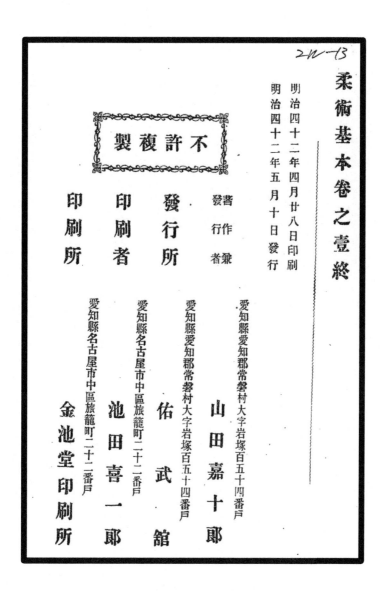

柔術基本卷之壹終

明治四十二年四月廿八日印刷
明治四十二年五月十日發行

不許複製

著作兼發行者　愛知縣愛知郡常磐村大字岩塚百五十四番戶　山田嘉十郎

發行所　愛知縣愛知郡常磐村大字岩塚百五十四番戶　佑武舘

印刷者　愛知縣名古屋市中區旅籠町二十二番戶　池田喜一郎

印刷所　愛知縣名古屋市中區旅籠町二十二番戶　金池堂印刷所

Jujutsu Kihon
Fundamentals of Jujutsu
Volume 1
End

Published in Aichi Prefecture
April 28th of Meiji 42 (1909)

145

乱捕活法柔術教科書

Randori ・ *Kappo*
Jujutsu ・ *Kyokasho*
**Free Sparring/
Resuscitation/
Jujutsu
Textbook**

Part I

- History
- Philosophy
- Uniform
- Stances
- Warm-up
- Basic Strikes
- Basic Grabs
- Chokes

井口義為
Inoguchi Yoshitame

1912

柔術教科書序

十八般の武藝は皆物具を要す獨り柔術に至ては一具の用なく赤手以て不慮の難に備ふるに足る要するに武術は一身の護りにして一國の護りたり鞁近武士道衰頽し又昔日の如くならず奢侈遊惰の潮流滔々として濫觴し殆んど底止する處を知らず豈長大息の至ならずや井口氏茲に憾あり以て此書を編す世の青年子

序

一

5423

148

Tajiri Inajiro 田尻 稲次郎 (1850 ~ 1923)

Jujutsu Kyokasho Jo
Foreword to the Jujutsu Textbook
By Tajiri Inajiro

Nearly all of the Bugei Juhappan, the 18 Martial Arts, require a weapon, however Jujutsu alone requires none. You simply fight "red-handed[9]" and use your bare hands to deal with an unexpected danger.

Though martial arts provide a means to defend yourself, of far greater importance is they allow you to protect your country. Recently Bushido, the way of the warrior, has been in decline in Japan, which is not at all like the days of old.

The new trend in society to immerse oneself in wave after wave of extravagance and indulgence shows no sign of abating.

---

[9] "Red-handed" is Sekishu 赤手 in Japanese. The first Kanji is the color red, but in this case it means "to show/ to bare"

弟業務の餘暇之を試み朝に習ひ夕に復し勤むる
の精に至らば斯道の妙處を會得せんこと一點の
疑を容れず請ふ許多の青年輩此書に依て柔道の
正路を踏み其身體を健全にし局面一轉尚武の氣
風を旺盛ならしめんことを茲に一言を記して以
て序と爲す

大正元年十月上旬

北雷狂夫識

Instead of simply sighing deeply at this deplorable state of affairs, Mr. Inoguchi has compiled this book to allow even young children to practice when they have completed their other duties.

By training in the morning and reviewing the material again in the evening, the lessons will permeate their psyche and they will become enlightened to the subtleties of this art.

Without a doubt this book will allow a great many young people to take their first steps on the path of proper Judo[10] training.

I write this foreword in the hope that as their bodies become healthy and strong we will have an outbreak of lively martial spirit.

Written in early October of the first year of Taisho (1912)

By Kitanari Kyofu[11] (Tajiri Inajiro)
"Crazy Man North Thunder"

---

[10] Throughout this book "Judo" and "Jujutsu" are used interchangeably.

[11] Tajiri, who gave himself the nickname "Crazy Man North Thunder" was from Satsuma Domain. From 1871~1879 he studied in America, attending a high school in Connecticut before attending Yale. He eventually got a master's degree in economics and public finance from Yale. He returned and worked for the government and later as the mayor of Tokyo.

自序

柳枝の風に靡くも折るゝこと無きは柔能く剛を制
するの理にして柔の奥儀も亦茲に基く故に柔道を
學ぶ者は須らく虚心平氣以て自然の理に從ひ日新
の工風を最も肝要とすべし予曩に吉田千春久富鐵
太郎齋藤明信等の先生と謀りし事の柔術劍道に關
する書數部を編し青年輩の獨學に便す頃日又諸彦
より亂捕法の書の著あらんことを望まるゝや切な
り然れども予歳既に耳順に達し燈下書を編するに

My Introduction
By Inoguchi Yoshitame 井口義為 (1852? ~ ?)

Just as the branches of a willow tree bend in the wind, but do not break, the soft and flexible can overcome the rigid. The principle is the same for both and reflects the deepest most fundamental part of Yawara[12].

It is essential for those who practice Judo to develop an understanding of this natural principle. To do this you must develop Kufu[13], or knacks, to improve yourself day by day as you train.

Over the past several years teachers such as Yoshida Chiharu, Hisatomi Tetsutaro and Saito Akinobu[14] have published books on Jujutsu and Kenjutsu. Over the course of several volumes they succeeded in creating resources for young people to do self-study in martial arts.

---

[12] Yawara is another way to read the Kanji 柔. Some Jujutsu schools refer to their art as Yawara, the soft and flexible way.

[13] Kufu are "tricks of the trade" a person develops. This word applies to any aspect of life not just martial arts.

[14] Yoshida Chiharu published:
An Illustrated Guide to the Essence of Tenjin Shinyo Ryu Jujutsu (1893)

Hisatomi Tetsutaro published:
A Police Officers Illustrated Guide to Kenpo (1888)

Saito Akinobu published:
The Illustrated Instructor's Guide to the Essence of Jikishin Kage Ryu Kenjutsu (1901)

自序

懶し辭するに若かずと已にして思へらく余命幾許
も無しと雖ども豈碌々として死を俟たん宜しく己
れの知得せるものを他人に示さば鈍刀亦一割の功
なからんやと茲に於て講道館及諸先生と謀り其術
は新を撰み實を取り其説明は煩を避け簡を旨とし
俗談平話一に會得し易からんことを要とし以て此
書を編す請ふ看官坊間に流布せる似而非的武術書
と一様の觀を爲すなからんことを

二

154

Recently however many accomplished people have approached me asking if I would write a book about how to do Randori, free sparring. However, since I am already 60 years old[15] it remains to be seen if I can slough off my laziness and properly draft a book by lamplight.

Though I do not have much life left to live, I would like to attempt to properly convey what I have learned to others so that I can die in peace. Though I am nothing but a dull sword, I feel I can make one more cut before I am rendered useless.

Thus just as the Kodokan and other martial arts instructors have done, I have re-evaluated techniques and selected the most effective. Further, I have endeavored to avoid complicated explanations and instead outline the essential points of each technique. Therefore this book will be written in the vernacular.

I have written this book using everyday language in order to allow the reader to easily absorb the material. My hope is that when it is distributed all over town and examined by readers they do not think this is one of the sham martial arts books that abound nowadays. [16]

---

[15] This is the only reference I could find to Inoguchi's age. If he was 60 in 1912, that means he was born around 1852.

When talking about his age, Inoguchi does not write the number 60 but uses the word "Obedient Ears." This is a reference to a line from the Analects by Confucius (551 ~479 BC.)

The Master said, "At fifteen, I had my mind bent on learning. "At thirty, I stood firm. "At forty, I had no doubts. "At fifty, I knew the decrees of Heaven. "At sixty, my ear was an obedient organ for the reception of truth. "At seventy, I could follow what my heart desired, without transgressing what was right."

-Translated by James Legge (1815-1897)

[16] Since this is a Jujutsu book by a man named Inoguchi, I presumed it was the son of Inoguchi Matsunosuke, who wrote *Fundamentals of Military Strategy*. However, it turns out Matsunosuke changed his name to Yoshitame, so both books are by the same author.

次序

今回予が著す處の柔術敎科書は本年議會に專習科に加へられた
るを以て今之に順序を立て初心の輩に示し更に亂捕の形を斯道
熱心者の爲に手を以て敎ふる如く圖畫を加へて說明し又呼吸術
より殺活方をも圖解にし中學校以上の學生其他の靑年輩の爲め
實地經驗の上にて梓に上し以て參考書とすされば各流派はあれ
ども皆大同小異なるを以て柔道の概略は此書により會得すべ
し尙又玆に洩れたるものは他日敎師用の書として之を著し又諸
流の形の書とも併せて發行せんと欲す本篇旣に云ふ如く斯道の
名人上手は漸々に故人となり古來の武術は殆んど有名無實に流
れ各流祖の功勞も將に消滅に歸せんとするは實に遺憾のことゝ
いふべし又古へより一子相傳の極意と稱し秘して人に傳へず徒
らに舊習を墨守せる者も亦なきにしも非らず是等は管に時世に
背くのみならず國家に忠ならざるもの也今や舊習一洗十八般の

自序

三

156

Second Introduction

This book, *The Jujutsu Textbook,* will be published following the decision by the Diet this year to include Judo as an official subject of study. This book will start with the basics for beginners. Later, for those who are dedicated practitioners, Randori Kata will be introduced with easy to understand illustrated explanations. Finally, there will be an illustrated guide to respiration techniques and resuscitation methods. This reference guide is intended to enable students that have already completed junior high school as well as other young people to gain practical knowledge that is applicable in life.

Though each school of Jujutsu has its own way of doing things there are all broadly the same and only vary in the details. Thus, everything you need to gain a basic understanding of the outline of Judo is within this book.

As to the sources used for this book, it is a compilation of other instructor's manuals as well as documents detailing how Kata are to be executed from all the other schools of Jujutsu. All this information was compiled into this volume.

Of late teachers at the pinnacle of this art are dying off one after another. This means the knowledge developed by the founders of these schools is being allowed to wash away rather ingloriously. This eradication of knowledge about old style martial arts is an unacceptable state of affairs.

Further, there are those who follow the old secret tradition of Isshin-soden. This means the most closely guarded secrets of a school are transmitted to only a single student. We can do without such ways as well as others who follow strict customs regarding how information is passed on. These people are not only ignoring the modern state of the world but are shirking their patriotic duty.

武藝の奧秘を明々白々說明し滿天下の青年輩をして武術の何た
るを解さしめ其體力を壯健にし皇國特有の日本魂を益々發揮し
一等國の名に背かざらんことを期し併せて各流祖の功勞に報は
ずんばあらず頃日德島縣川口郡柿原村松下某より關口流の秘訣
古書を寄送されたるを本とし各流秘術の寄書を合し不日世間に
紹介の勞を取らんと欲す

大正元年十月

免許

義

爲識

158

What I am attempting to do is sweep aside the old secrecy and bring into the light the deepest held secrets found within the 18 Martial Arts. By clearly explaining all aspects of these arts, including what was heretofore secret, all the youth under the heavens can understand the purpose and inner meaning of martial arts. They will develop strength and become healthy and my hope is that, through this Yamato Damashi, the spirit of the ancient Japanese warrior particular to Imperial Japan, will manifest itself in greater and greater strength. The youth will not shirk their duty to maintain the honor of our supreme country.

To the credit of many heads of martial arts schools, I recently received a package from Tokushima Prefecture. The package from Mr. Matsushita Shall-Not-Be-Named of Kashiwahara Village in the Kawaguchi Region contained an old secret document from the Sekiguchi School of Jujutsu.

I have made this into a book and combined the secret techniques of all the schools of Jujutsu from documents donated to me. I hope to be able to introduce the fruits of my labors to the public in short order.

Written in October of the First Year of the Taisho Emperor (1912)
Menkyo Rank Holder
Yoshitame

亂捕活法 柔術教科書

免許　柳松齋　井口義爲著

柔術の起源

凡そ柔術は支那に起りて我國に傳りしものなるべし。去れはに明の萬歷年中に刊行せる萬法全書中にも、劍・鉾・槍・棒・弓・柔術等の圖畫を加たる者あり。我朝にては天文年中作州津山波賀村の人竹内中務大輔久盛なる者此術を修練し、小具足捕手と號け、遂に一派を開く、之を竹内流と云ふ。久盛修驗道を以て諸國を遍歷し到處に此術を教授し、子孫にも亦之を傳へり。今猶中國筋にては往々此流の形を見ることあり。其後永祿年間支那より陳元賓と云ふ者來り武州江戸現今の東京麻布の國正寺に寓居し此術を敎ふ事

柔術の起源

一

160

Randori & Resuscitation: A Jujutsu Textbook
By Menkyo License "Yanagi Shosai" Inoguchi Yoshitame
The Origins of Jujutsu

It is well known that Jujutsu originated in China and was later transmitted to our country. During the reign of the 14th Ming Emperor, known as the Banreki Emperor (1563 ~ 1620) a volume known as *The Book of Ten Thousand Methods* was published.[17] This book contained chapters with illustrated descriptions of how to use swords, halberds, spears, staff, shoot a bow or crossbow as well as Jujutsu.

In our imperial land, during the Tenbun Era (1532 ~ 1555) there was a man named Takenouchi Nakatsukasadaiyu Hisamori who lived in Tsuyamahaga Village, Sakushu Domain. He rigorously studied these techniques and developed a method he called Kogusoku Torite[18]. This later formed the base of his school, which he called Takenouchi Ryu. Hisamori then travelled to all parts of the country in a martial arts pilgrimage that became legendary. By the time he had finished he had transmitted his art to many people and his decedents continue to pass on his martial arts technique. Even today in China you can see similar techniques being done that originated from the same source.

---

[17] I was unable to locate book, or even a reference to a book called *The Book of Ten Thousand Methods*. Mr. Inoguchi is probably referring to either:

New Treatise on Military Efficiency 紀效新書 (1560) by Seki Keiko

or

Treatise on Armament Technology 武備志 (1621) by Mao Yuanyi.

The latter book is known as the *Bubishi* in Japan. Both of these books contain extensive illustrated instructions on weapons and military strategy.

[18] Kogusoku refers to either armed close combat in light armor or grappling using short edged weapons such as a Wakizashi or a Tanto. Torite is a term used by some schools to denote offensive unarmed tactics, where the objective is to restrain and arrest or kill the enemy. This later evolved into more self-defense oriented unarmed combat techniques seen in Jujutsu.

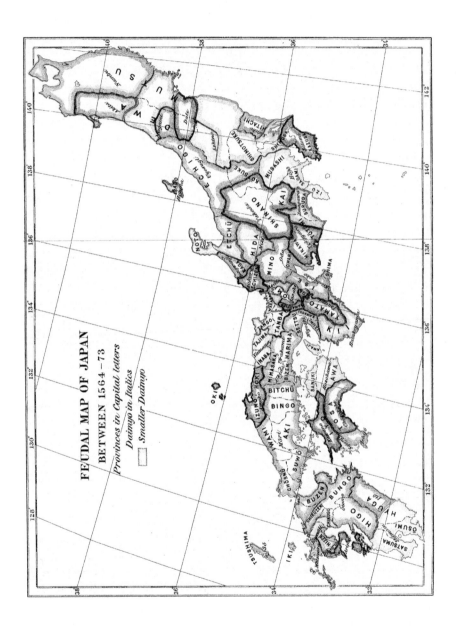

Chin Genpin 陳元贇 (1587—1671)

Later in the Kanei Era (1624 ~ 1644) a man named Chin Genpin came to Edo City in Bushu Domain. Today this place is the Azabu part of Tokyo.[19] He stayed at Kokusho Temple and taught Chinese Kenpo to three Samurai: Miura Yoshitatsu, Fukuno Masakatsu and Isogai Jiro Saemon. Each became enlightened to the inner mysteries of this art. Eventually Miura and Fukuno mastered the art sufficiently and they wrapped this new way of teaching around their core of knowledge of Jujutsu and set off to spread their new school across Japan.

---

[19] In the spring of 1621 Chin Genpin was part of a government mission from China to Japan to protest the raids by Wako Japanese pirates on the eastern coast of China. He is credited with introducing either Kenpo, Jujutsu or both to Japan.

An anonymous work, Kenpo Hisho 拳法秘書*, published sometime before 1683, stated that Jujutsu had originated in Japan following a conversation between Chin and three Ronin regarding the "Chinese method of seizing a man." This theory has since been widely accepted....Chin probably should not be regarded as the founder of Jujutsu, but rather as one who gave it the stimulus that inspired its later prodigious development. He died in 1761 and his remains were interred at the Kenchu monastery in Nagoya.*

-Eminent Chinese of the Qing Period: 1644-1911/2
Edited by Arthur W. Hummel Sr.

柔　術　教　科　書

柔術大意

三浦義辰、福野正勝、磯貝次郎左衞門の三氏其門に入り各々奧儀を極む、殊に三浦、福野の如きは遂に一機軸を出し別に一派を編出して之を世に擴む。是れ我朝に於て中古柔術の祖と傳稱す。其門人漸次增加して各自一派を開き即ち現今に於ては三四十の流派あり。然して其の亂捕に至りては大抵他派と試合を爲すも劍道の面胴、小手、突と云ふ如く、又書道を學ぶに初めいろはを以てすると同じく殆んど同一の形を演ず又柔道亂捕にては腰、手、足、締逆の業を多く用ふるにより後進者に是等の形を圖に示し以て一般の教科書と爲せり。されば苟も此道に志ある者は必ず之を熟讀翫味し、之に就て學び怠らざるときは現時勇名を轟かせる講道館の八段横山作次郎、山下義昭兩氏の如き技量に至らざるの理なしと心得べし。餘は教師用の著書に明記す。

In our imperial country Chin Genpin is considered to be the one who inspired the revival of Jujutsu in the middle period of our history.[20] The students of these schools rapidly increased and each of them in turn began their own branches, and nowadays we have 30 or 40 different schools.

It is important to note that Randori, free sparring, was primarily something done when dueling with members of other schools. While Kendo has the standard strikes Men, Doh, Kote, Tsuki and calligraphy starts by learning to write your A,B,C's. Jujutsu matches, on the other hand, would not be employing the same Kata every time.

In short, Jujutsu Randori has many techniques that require the use of the hips, hands and feet as well as chokes and joint locks. In order to make a general textbook for the next generation of Jujutsu practitioners, illustrations will accompany the descriptions of the Kata. That way, if someone has even the slightest desire to start down this path they can develop an appreciation for this art by reading this book thoroughly. Then, if they study and train according to these principles, their fame will begin to thunder out. The breadth of their skill will become as famous as the 8th Dan Kodokan Judoka Mr. Yokoyama Sakujiro and Mr. Yamashita Yoshiaki.

There will be a further discussion of this in the instructor's volume.

---

[20] Volume 10 of the *Bugei Shoden* (*A Short History of Martial Arts In Japan,*) written in 1714 by Hinatsu Yasuke 日夏弥助 a Tendo School practitioner contains a chapter on unarmed fighting. The chapter is titled Ken 拳(fist, not sword) and the first few lines are:

According to Secrets of the Fist what is known nowadays as Jujutsu or Yawara was called Ken, the fist, in the Bubishi 武備志. Long ago in Japan these techniques were known as Shuhaku, or Hand Specialist. In the early Edo period Chin Genpin came to Japan and stayed in Edo.

柔術敎科書

柔術の大意は柔能く剛を制するの理にして武術中一種特別の技術なり故に此理を會得するときは彼劍術の如く木刀、竹刀面胴、小手の道具を用ひず赤裸無手只自體四肢の活動に依り如何なる剛強の者に出會するも直に之を取つて押へることを得るの術たり。されば常に此道を研磨して時に臨んで不覺を取らざる様にすべし。倘て此道を學ぶには男女を問はず十二三歳より二十六歳迄の間を以て最も適當の期なりとす、故に初め此書に依り稽古を爲すこと久しき時は自然と悟り得るなり。

文運日に進み大平の恩澤に浴する今日といへども惡漢等に出遇ふこと無しとも計り難し故に人々は充分此術を會得し身體を健全にし其機に臨み能く敵を制し不意の凶事を防禦するは最も肝要なることゝ知るべし。

柔能く剛を制するの理由

柔能く剛を制するの理由

三

The Fundamental Concept of Jujutsu

The fundamental meaning of Jujutsu lies with the principle that the soft and flexible can control the strong and rigid. Though Jujutsu is part of martial arts in general, it is a special art. This is because unlike Kenjutsu you do not use Bokuto (wooden swords,) Shinai (bamboo swords,) Men (helmets,) Kote (hand-guards) or other protective gear or implements. Instead you are Seki-Ra-Mu-Te, completely naked,[21] with nothing in your hands. This art teaches you to employ your body and four limbs in order to immediately assume control over any strong and rigid opponent you may encounter. Thus, anyone who has trained this way diligently will not be caught unaware.

Ideally, training should start around 12 or 13 years old. This applies to both boys and girls. From then until about 26 years old is the period when the most progress will be made. Whenever you decide to begin the training regimen contained in this document, this fact will naturally become apparent over time.

As you advance in this art on a daily basis, enjoying the benefits of this peaceful age, remember that there is no guarantee you will not encounter some ruffian or violent person. Thus, I encourage all people to develop skill in the art of Jujutsu, which will not only help your body become healthy but allow you to easily control an opponent if suddenly faced with a dangerous situation. Understand that the fundamental benefit of this art is to protect yourself from unexpected danger.

---

[21] "Completely naked" probably also refers to being unarmored.

柔 術 敎 科 書

柔道の形を學ぶを必要とする事

柔術を會得し得る時は如何なる剛敵無法に出遇時も決して怖るるの念を生ぜず心神沈着にして亂れざる故に其敵に打勝つものなり。又一見敵の形狀弱きに見ゆることもあるも決して侮り輕んずべからず先づ敵に如何なる技量あるかを知ることを肝要とす、されば常に其業を練磨して其妙味を解する時は假令多勢の惡漢又は強敵に出遇ふも單身能く之を制することを得るものなり。假令は大船の水上に行くが如く數人の乘客あるも一人舵機を操つる時は其の欲する處に到達し得るが如し。柔道は亦多數の強敵あるも只一人にて之を操ることは舟子の舵機を操つると同一の理なりと知るべし。然れども是を施すに於ては其術の巧拙に係るなれば常に怠らず專心其技を研究すべし。

柔道の形を學ぶを必要とする事

柔道も亦流派あり其流儀に依つて必ず其流儀の形有斯道の元祖

The Reason the Soft and Flexible Overcomes the Strong and Rigid

So what will happen after you become knowledgeable about Jujutsu? If you should encounter a fierce and completely lawless person, fear will not well up inside you. Your spirit will remain calm and your body relaxed. Since you have not been thrown into a panic, you will be able to strike him down and win.

However, even if your opponent does not seem to be particularly strong, never underestimate him. You have no idea the range of techniques he may possess. This is an essential point, which is why you should extensively train and polish your Jujutsu techniques until you have developed an understanding of the subtleties of the art. By doing so, even if you are alone and faced with a group of villains or a single powerful opponent, you will be able to control them.

To put this in perspective, imagine there is a large boat floating on the water. While there may be many people on board, the one controlling the rudder decides where he wants to land the boat. Understand that Judo works the same way. Even if you are faced with many strong opponents, you can, by yourself control the situation just as if you were using a rudder to adjust the course of a craft on water. The principle is the same.

However, in order to become able to handle situations in such a manner you must first become adept in this art. The key to becoming skilled is to never be lax in your training and devote yourself entirely to learning and refining your technique.

柔術教科書

と稱せらるゝ人は種々他流の形を見、或は教導口授を受けて遂に

一流を組立つるものなり。即ち天神眞楊流の元祖磯又右衞門先

生は始め楊心流を學び次に眞之神道流を合して一機軸を出し遂

に天神眞楊流と號する一派を弘む。又楊心流元祖は長崎の人に

て秋山四郎兵衞と曰ひて小兒科の醫師なりしが醫學修業の爲め

支那に渡りし際博轉と云ふ支那人に就きて柔術の形三手を學び

得たり。

當時支那に於ては唯蹴ると突くとの形を專門とし日本の柔術

とは大に違へり。秋山氏は僅かに三手の柔術形を熟練し更に活

生法二十八種の傳授を受け歸朝の後之を人に傳授す然れども其

手形少なき故を以て練習する者大抵半途にして廢止す。秋山氏

大に之を歎き筑紫太宰府の菅廟に祈願を罩めて形手の工風を凝

らし遂に三百三手を編み出したりと云ふ。又神廟の前に柳の大

樹有り大雪の際に其枝に雪の積まざるを感悟して遂に楊心流と

柔道の形を學ぶな必要とする事

五

The Reason You Have to Learn Judo Kata

There are many different schools of Judo and each school has its own particular philosophy. The founder of each school has invariably developed his own particular Kata and way of teaching by observing Kata from countless other schools. He may have even received direct instruction from some of them. In the end, he has compiled all this information and founded his own school.

An example of this is the founder of Tenjin Shinyo Ryu, Isomata Emon Sensei. Isomata Sensei first studied Yoshin Ryu and then he merged his knowledge of that school with Shinnoshindo Ryu. In the end he developed an entirely new school, which he called Tenjin Shinyo School, which began to spread all over Japan.

The founder of the Yoshin School was a man from Nagasaki named Akiyama Shirobe. He was a pediatrician and to improve his technique Akiyama Sensei traveled to China for study. While he was there Akiyama met a Chinese man named Hakuden who taught him three Jujutsu Kata.

At the time, Chinese Kata were completely different from Japanese Jujutsu since they contained primarily kicks and punches. Akiyama Sensei trained intensely but mastered just 3 Chinese Jujutsu Kata. In addition he received complete transmission of 28 different kinds of resuscitation techniques. When Akiyama Sensei returned to his homeland he began to teach these techniques, however since there were so few techniques his students tended to quit and he eventually abandoned his school. Akiyama Sensei was very distressed by this turn of events and went to the Dazaifu Tenman Shinto Shrine in Fukuoka Prefecture, which is dedicated to the scholar and poet Sugawara no Michizane (845 ~ 903.) He went to the tomb of the Michizane, who is known as Tenjin, the Shinto god of learning, and asked for guidance.

It is said he was inspired and trained and experimented before developing 303 techniques. Further, there was a willow tree in front of the mausoleum. One day, after a snowstorm, he noticed how the snow did not build up on the branches. This caused him to name his school Yoshin Ryu or "Spirit of the Willow Tree School."

柔　術　敎　科　書

號する一派を開く。

と云ふ人此楊心流を學び亦工風を凝し分別して流名に上中下三段の級を定め其手數六十八手として一派を開く。之を眞の神道流と號す。磯氏の如きも亦之と同じ。現今加納治五郎先生も天神眞楊流を學び後に起到流を吉田直藏先生に學び今講道舘流を弘めたり。

柔術は形が必要なる事亂捕は劍術で云ふ道具を着けて面、小手、胴突と云ひ文字に喩ふれば草書の如きものなり。都而何業も眞行草と三段に學ぶを宜とす。其の亂捕も形種々あり著者以て全體に勝貧を附けるものなり。他流試合は亂捕を圖解を示して一般後進者に便利を與へんが爲めに記するものな

又神道流元祖は大阪城の同心山本民左衛門

六

り。

武藝進歩に附三毒の心得

In addition, the founder of Shindo School was a Dojin, police assistant, who worked at Osaka Castle named Yamamoto Tamizaeman. He studied the aforementioned Yoshin School and continued to refine and devise new elements. Eventually, he divided all the techniques in this school into three categories : Upper, Middle and Lower. Having made these three levels he formed his school around 68 techniques. Yamamoto called his school Shin-no-shindo Ryu. In other words, he did exactly what Mr.Iso did long ago. These days Kano Jigoro Sensei, who was a student of Tenjin Shinyo School and later Kito school under Yoshida Naozo Sensei has begun to spread his Kodokan School of Jujutsu.

Kata are essential to Jujutsu. Randori in Kendo means you put on protective gear and strike to Men (the head) and Kote (the hands) and stab to Doh (the body.) For writing, it is like calligraphy.

All Kata training should be done according to the three-category Shingyoso system. Shingyoso is a term that originally referred to different ways of writing Kanji. Kanji can be written in three ways: printed, semi-cursive, and cursive styles. However, Shingyoso evolved into a three-category system used in all traditional disciplines, including martial arts. The three categories are: basic, halfway, and transformed.[22]

When you are doing Taryujiai, or dueling with members from another school, you will be using Randori. Achieving victory or being defeated depends on how you apply these techniques with your entire body. There are many kinds of Randori Kata and I will be introducing them with illustrated explanations so that they will be easy to grasp for the following generation.

---

[22] In addition to calligraphy, Shingyoso 真行草 the three category system, can be found in everything from Kenjutsu and Hojo rope-binding to garden-path making and room design.

凡そ愼む可きものは三毒成なり。

三毒と云ふは即ち酒色財なり第一酒に心亂れては稽古不充分なるは勿論他に種々の危險を生ず。又色慾に迷ひ博奕等を爲すが如きは惰弱に流れ自然心亂るが故に此の三界を愼みて熱心に修業すべし。此柔術と云ふは人を害するものにあらず第一は護身の爲め運動及身體強壯に成るが爲めに學ぶものなり。

酒に醉ふて他人に害を加へ色慾に狂ひて婦女子に亂暴を加へ。又は柔術を亂用して他人を驚かすが如き行爲は一切有らざる樣愼むべし。

總て藝術には上に上のあるものにて之れにて宜しと云ふことなければ成るべく上手の者に教を乞ひ充分先輩の妙手を覺へんと心掛けて稽古をすることを第一とす。常に上手の者に稽古を賴みて自身にも亦技を研究して後進者に教傳するを上手と云ふ。

他人の稽古を見て其妙手を取りて我が短所を補ふ樣心掛くべし、自身何程上達せりとも上に上ある喩への通りなるが故に人間一

How Improve Your Martial Arts
Caution About The Three Poisons

The things you should be most careful about are the Three Poisons. The Three Poisons are alcohol, lust and gambling. It goes without saying that the first, alcohol, puts your spirit in a jumble, which prevents you from training effectively. Further, you can end up in all kinds of dangerous situations. Next, being obsessed with sexual satisfaction or gambling will naturally cause you to become physically weak and mentally lazy. Thus you should ignore these three realms and focus your passion on training.

The purpose of Jujutsu is not to injure people. The primary reason you are studying it is self-defense. You will achieve this by exercising to forge a strong and healthy body. Consuming alcohol and becoming intoxicated could result in you injuring another person. If lust addles your mind you may end up doing violence to a woman. Jujutsu is not to be used indiscriminately in order to impress and amuse those nearby. Be mindful of never allowing these three conditions to occur.

The goal of any art is to continuously improve and progress. If you do to think you are making good progress, ask a skilled practitioner to teach you. Make one of your primary goals during training to learn the subtleties you see in your Senpai's technique. You should endeavor, as a matter of course, to ask to train with skilled practitioners. Becoming skilled means that you then take what you learn and teach it to those who will follow you on the path. This is how you become good at Jujutsu.

Your goal should be to watch how others train and seize the subtle elements you observe. Then work those elements into your training to overcome areas you are weak. Though you may become an expert, you must still to advance and improve, as you continue on the path of Jujutsu. It is training that will take your whole lifetime.

生が稽古なりと心得べし。

術を學ぶの心得．

柔術敎科書

柔術を學ぶ者は稽古前には大食飲酒を堅く愼むべし。大食をし
て稽古を爲す時は必ず身體に害あり投げられ到れし時嘔吐を催
すことあり。嘗て初代磯先生の道場の寒稽古の時は毎朝四時頃
より門人寒稽古を爲すに當り何も食はず七八時の頃稽古を休み
水四升餘の處へ白米六七合を入れて三時間餘を炊きたる粥二椀
づゝ位を食したるものなりと云ふ。今は右樣なる稽古を爲す必
用なきも常に其心得を以て稽古に當り大食せざる樣心掛くべし。
稽古を爲すにも力量有るに任せ力を罩めて突張り強情になす時
は術の術たる所を會得すること出來難く外の條に示す如く心を
柳の枝の如く四肢は成べく柔かく動かし腰に力を入れて業を掛け
る刹那に下腹四肢に力を罩め電光の如き早業を掛ける時は敵は

八

How to Study Jutsu (Techniques)

For those that are studying Jujutsu, remember that you should absolutely refrain from eating a large meal or drinking Sake before training. If you eat a large meal before training, it will invariably lead to bodily harm. When you are thrown or knocked down you will feel as if you are going to throw up.

When Iso Sensei, the first-generation head, had Kangeiko, cold weather training, at his Dojo, the students all arrived at 4am. They would start cold-weather Jujutsu training without eating anything and continue until 7 or 8 o'clock. Then Iso Sensei would put 4 Sho, about 7.2 liters of water in a cauldron and add 6 or 7 Go, 600 ~ 1050 grams of polished short grain rice. This would be boiled for 3 hours, and when it was done each student could have up to two bowls of Kayu, rice porridge.

Though nowadays it is not necessary to train in such a fashion, you should always train with this philosophy in mind.

The tendency to rely on strength in training and, in particular, stubbornly continue to attack powerfully will prevent you from developing an understanding of what makes a technique a technique. In addition, as was mentioned before, your spirit should be pliant as the branches of a willow tree. Keep your limbs flexible as you move and put power in your hips. At the crucial moment you are applying a technique, focus all your power in the spot below your abdomen and apply your technique as fast as lightning. If you train this way, your opponent will surely be thrown in dramatic fashion.

When you are receiving direct instruction from your Sensei, be sure not to allow your body to become stiff. Going rigid will prevent you from understanding the subtleties of the technique being taught and can frequently leads to injury.

In addition, if you drink Sake before training you will end up with the same problems as overeating before training. Be aware that from days long past there have been many warriors that destroyed their bodies from drinking Sake to excess.

柔術教科書

見事に投げらるゝものなり。
すべからず然らざれば術の妙味を會得せずして自身に怪我を受
くる事多し。又飲酒して稽古する時は大食の時と同様の害あり
と知るべし。
往昔著名の武術者にして大酒の爲に身を亡したる例枚擧に暇
あらず心すべきことなり。

氣の滿つる事

氣の滿つると云ふ事は常に氣の弛み心撓む事なく弓を張りたる
如くにして中心を正しく座する處を氣の滿つると云ふ。譬へば
摩利支天像の如く蓋し心一なりと雖ども能く其心の六手に行渡
りたるが故に皆一同に動き働くを得るなり若し心が一方に偏倚
る時は必ず動く手と動かぬ手と有るに至る動かざるに於ては幾
本有りても用をなさず是にては氣の滿つるとは云ひ難し故に頭

氣の滿つる事

九

How to Maximize Your Energy

The way to maximize your Ki, or energy, is to ensure your concentration does not slacken and your awareness remains constant. Your mind should be centered firmly allowing you to pull it tight like an archer drawing his bow. This is how you keep yourself fully infused with martial energy. For example, when you look a statue of Marishiten[23] you realize her spirit is truly unified throughout her form. It is apparent that Marishiten's energy permeates each of her six hands and it is because of this, she is able to move each of them to perform actions.

If all her energy is concentrated in one hand, then she would have one hand performing an action while the others were not moving.

---

[23] Marishi Sonten 摩利支尊天 is the Deva or Bodhisattva of the light and the sun. Samurai invoked the female deity Marishiten to achieve victory since Marici means "light" or "mirage." Prayers to her would enable Samurai to escape the notice of their enemies.

Image of Marishiten from a Yoshin School Densho

柔　術　敎　科　書

より手足の先に至る迄能く氣の行き届き行渡りて一點の間隙なく平生充分に正しく安坐する處の有樣を以て氣の滿つると云ふなり是眞の位の第一と云ふ意なり。て六手の動くの意なり武術も之を悟らば自然四肢も充分動き得べし是れ即ち氣の滿るにあり。

摩利支天の像は一軆三面に

一〇。

氣と軆との事

氣と軆と云の中に陰陽あり則ち軆中に存する氣の起りを陽と云ひ亦其靜まるを陰と云ふ柔術に於て專ら氣の扱ひ方を敎へて業を成さしむると雖も之れ無形物にして外面に露出せるものにあらず唯軆中に滿ち存する處陰陽なれば隨つて弥み撓みて全から

ざる事あり。平常安座したる處の心氣は漫々として所謂愼靜無事の姿なれ共動作を始め身體手足を運用爲すに至れば其業に從つて中心傾き終に平常の氣を損するものなり。故に昔日柔術

In such a situation, despite having multiple hands, the majority are not being used. If you were in such a state it would be difficult to say your martial energy had infused every part of your body.

Thus, you should ensure your energy is distributed from the top of your head to the bottoms of your feet and all spots in between, without any gaps. If your energy is spread out and fills your whole body, and you are maintaining a calm, everyday state of mind, then you can be said to be maximizing your martial energy.

This is the meaning of Shin no Kurai, the True Stance Kamae. The reason a Marishiten statue has 1 body, 3 faces and 6 hands is because she can use all of them. If we apply this to when we are doing martial arts, it means your body is completely infused with energy and, being aware of your whole body, you will naturally become able move freely.

Energy and Your Body

Yin and Yang, darkness and light, are part of your body and martial energy. What this means is that the Ki, or energy, you produce in your body is Yang, light. And the stillness is Yin, darkness. In Jujutsu the way you are taught to use your energy to perform Waza, however this process is shapeless and cannot be shown externally. The Yin and Yang are within the body, filling it up completely. Thus, it is imperative you do not allow your spirit to slacken or your concentration to falter.

You should maintain your mind in a calm, everyday state, while keeping your energy maximized in every part of your body. This state is known as *Tranquil and Taking no Action*. However, when you begin an action with your body, hands, or feet your mind focuses on the movements of that Waza, thereby disrupting your tranquil, everyday mind. Thus, from days long past, when the head of a Jujutsu school transmitted the inner secrets of his art, he always ensured a student had developed a sufficient capacity to generate energy and maintain it without slackening or becoming distracted by a thing or a person.

You should not allow your mind, and the energy created by your body, to stop on anything.   At the same time you should be strictly adhering to the fundamental point of all the 10,000 techniques that exist.

柔　術　教　科　書

家に於て秘傳と爲したる處必ず先づ己が方寸の元氣を養ひ弛み怠らしめず事物に心氣を停むる事なく宜く萬業の基本たる處を堅固に保ち守らしむるを要すと基本既に定つて業を爲せば如何程働き動くとも元氣能く決して缺損する事なし左に力を用ふるも右の空しき事なく亦右を働かすも左弛まず前後上下に隙なくして起居動靜共に氣を損する無きに至れば眞に大丈夫と云ふ可きなり。此の咄種々あり教師用に著はす。

志と氣と力との事

志氣力の此三つは區別して論ずる事甚だ以て難しと然れ共今試に之を分けて云へば眼前に或一物在り是を取らんとする志の起るに隨ふて手の前へ出るは何ぞや是れ志に隨つて氣の手に通ふが故にして其物を取り扱ふは即ち氣に隨つて力の手に集るに由るなり。又力の出づる處には氣集り氣の通ふ處には力集る事は

志と氣と力との事

二

If you are able to execute the fundamentals of a Waza, then no matter how difficult the opponent your movements will be vigorous and your technique will not fail you at the critical moment.

If you are putting power into the left side of your body, your right side does not become a void. If you are moving your right your left does not slacken. There are no gaps in front, behind, left or right. It does not matter whether you are standing, sitting, moving or still, your energy is not affected. If you achieve this state then you can truly say that you are a powerful warrior. There are many other talks related to this which I will include for instructors.

Shi, Ki, Chikara
Will, Energy and Power

Though quite difficult, I would like to explain how to differentiate between Will, Energy and Power. To start with, say there is something in front of your eyes that you want to seize. Your Will is activated and your hand moves forward, but why does that happen? This is because your Energy has been activated by your Will and passed to your hand. Next, your Energy directs the Power you have focused in your hand, and causes your hand to grip the object or person.

Thus Power is released when your Energy is gathered in one point. The principle at work here is that your Energy has to flow in order for you to focus on your Power. Energy and Power are two sides of the same coin.

However, if you try to employ a Waza by just using Power, then you will be putting yourself in a lot of danger. Therefore you should abandon using Power in training and focus on developing your ability to control your Energy. So, if you want to become expert at using Waza, you need to be able to adapt your technique to the particular Power each opponent possesses, then control the release of your Power according to that person. It is clear this way of thinking should be taught from the very beginning.

Thus the essence of this lesson is you should unify your Will, Energy and Power since they are all inseparable.

柔術敎科書

弱身強壯に成るは柔術にあり

一定の理にして氣力不二となるものなり。然れども力を先立て
て業を爲せば其害甚だ多し即ち力を捨て唯氣の扱ひを熟練せし
めんが爲めなりとす故に業熟達するに至れば人々固有の力は其
業に應じ働きに隨ふて出づる事は固より敎へを待たずして明か
なり。されば志氣,力を合一するを以て不二の妙處なりとす。

弱身強壯に成るは柔術にあり

弱身の者は幼時より此の道に入れ置く時は身體の發育上を充分
ならしめ體力自然に備はり且つ術を修め業を鍛練せば勝負の實
地に克く勝を制するを得べく延いては智德も進みて利益多し臆
病なる者又は婦女子と雖も運動の爲めに常に幼時より斯道に入
れ置けば氣を養ひ心を廣く持つ事を得べく極めて有益なり。最
も初めは其の身に適する丈けを學ぶものなれば過劇なる運動に
はあらざるなり,自分の身體に適する位の練習が後に至り大に

二.

For Those Weak of Body, The Key to Becoming Strong is Jujutsu

Those with weak bodies should start on the path of Jujutsu training from a young age. As your body grows, you will naturally develop strength. Further, if you learn this art and train Waza extensively you will be able to easily achieve victory in a real-life situation. It will also improve your knowledge and virtue in addition to many other benefits.

If you are a bit cowardly or a girl, woman or housewife and adopt this exercise, it will develop your energy and improve your mental health. Jujutsu exercise is an extremely beneficial course of study. Initially, you should only train as appropriate to your body. When you begin learning Jujutsu it is not necessary to exercise to an extreme degree. Rather, adjust your training level to suit your body you will reap great rewards. By training in this manner, you will develop an understanding of how to learn Waza. For Japanese boys this will of course serve to develop Bushi Seishin, warrior spirit. Wives, women and girls will become able to fend off an attack if suddenly faced with a violent person and emerge uninjured. Thus it will serve as a method of self-defense when faced with an emergency.

As the fathers and elder brothers of the world move on,
Their children and younger siblings should begin on this path,
This way is followed by courageous warriors for our honored
country and parents,
Polish your spirit for your decedents

Yoshitame

柔術敎科書

利益を得るなり。

斯くして身體の發育に随ひ好みで業を學ぶ様に成るものなり。

日本男子として武士的精神を養ふは勿論婦女子と云へども亂暴者に出遇ひいかなる害を受けぬ限りもあらず

萬一の際は護身の術となるなり。

世の父兄は進んで子弟を斯道に入れ給ふべきことなり。

一つはものは御國と親の爲めなるぞ末のためなり

こゝろみがけよ

義爲

武術に免許皆傳と云ふ事

凡そ何武藝に於ては免許皆傳と云ふ事あり。

警視廳講道館の外は師匠、先生の意に叶ひ次第に業の妙處を自得せるものには最初折紙を渡し。師より門人一同へ此度何某は折紙の腕あり依て是を渡すと申渡すなり後數年を經て形及亂捕の奥儀を極めるに至り口傳秘傳の免狀を渡すなりそれ目今警視廳にて定めし三級に

武術に免許皆傳と云ふ事

一三

Menkyo Kaiden in Martial Arts

Nearly all marital arts use a license system called Menkyo Kaiden, which is a certificate of complete transmission of all aspects of a school's teachings. The police department, the Kodokan as well as the heads of other schools grant certification when they deem a student has achieved a certain degree of proficiency, subtlety and beauty in their Waza.

Typically the first rank is Origami, Folded Paper. The Sensei granting this license would typically present the certificate in front of all the other students by saying, "Recently so-and-so has demonstrated abilities equivalent Origami and I hereby grant him this license."

Then, several years later, when the student has become enlightened to the Okuden, or inner mysteries of Kata as well as Randori, a Kuden Hiden, or Oral Transmission Secret Teachings, license would be granted. This is roughly equivalent to the Sankyu, Three Level, system used by the police department.

The actual document handed over is a Maki-mono, or scroll. The number of scrolls issued depends on the school. One common way they arranged is Ken-Kon, or Heaven and Earth, scrolls. Another way is dividing the information among three scrolls Ten-Chi-Jin, or Heaven-Earth-Human.

In our Shinyo Ryu, when a license is awarded the student receives 4 scrolls, though depending on the school the number of scrolls and the way their Gokui, or Ultimate Secrets, are awarded can vary considerably. For the most part, however, schools use the Heaven-Earth-Human progression to license complete transmission. You should understand that other martial arts generally follow the same pattern.

Among all martial arts, Judo is the newest fighting art and is expanding vigorously. All the Judo instructors you find working in various prefectures were all formerly students of Jujutsu schools who received license in that art from their teacher. Finally, with regards to Meijin, Famous People, understand that this is not a title a person would call themselves. Instead it refers to a person in any industry who is deemed superior to others in their field. Nowadays there are probably only 2 or 3 such people around.

柔術教科書

相當するものなり此の免許に渡す卷物に乾坤の二卷に為すも有り又天地人三卷と為すもあり我が眞楊流は四卷を授くるものなり

るが極意に依りて種々の渡し方あるも大概は天地人皆傳と云ふ。諸武藝中柔道が一番

他の武藝にても全般同一の事と知るべし。新らしき武術にて現今は柔術が最も隆盛を極むるなり。各府縣

下に在住せる柔道教師は皆昔より師の傳を受けて今に至るもの

なり。又名人と云ふは自身に言ふにあらず何業にても人々に勝れたるものを指して名人と云ふ當今名人と言はるゝ人は二三人

位に過ぎざるべし。

一心と云ふ事

總じて物事には一心に成るべし神道の金光教にも一心に信心せよ御蔭は我が心にありと云ふことあり。昔より武術修業者は神

に祈りて一派一流を起したる者澤山あり奥を極めて一心不亂に

Isshin : Devoting Yourself Completely

No matter what activity you are engaged in, you should devote yourself entirely to it. There is a type of Shinto called Konkokyo[24], Teachings of the Golden Light, that I have committed myself to and it has allowed me to find my spirit.

Long ago martial artists doing ascetic training would pray to a deity for inspiration, many of them would go on to establish their own branch or school of war.

Those that train in an art single-mindedly and without interruption until they have become enlightened to the inner mysteries are the one whose names are remembered. In particular, study related to fighting requires your spirit to permeate all aspects of the art. This is of primary importance.

Graciously, we have a song left to us by a previous emperor,

Using a pole to guide a boat along, without being aware of your actions,
Your small boat slips between the reeds,
The rain forms a hollow in a rock after pouring off the eve of the roof,
Think of this as the most difficult Waza

What this is saying is, once boys begin something, they should continue studying it until they have discovered its inner mysteries.

---

[24] Konkokyo 金光教 is a Shinto sect. Konkokyo adherents worship primarily the spirit and energy that flows through all things, called *Tenchi Kane No Kami*, or the Golden Kami of the Heavens and Earth. It was founded by Kawate Bunjiro Kawate 川手文治郎 (1814~1883) in 1859.

柔術敎科書

稽古を爲す者は何藝に於ても世に名を著はすものなり。

殊に武術的のものは猶更の事にて一心を貫く事第一なり。

畏くも先帝陛下の大御歌に

とる棹のこゝろなかくも漕ぎ寄せむ

葦間の小舟さはりありとも

雨たりにくゝほみし軒の石みても

かたき業とて思ひすてめや

男子一度起たば何事も其の奥を極むるまで學べかし進めよかし。

と云ふ御意味なり。

無我無心の位の事

凡そ見處のものをば直に其相手取る氣に成り形を造るは其處へ心を留るものにして是は我が心に好を求る處有るが故なり又隨つて敵あるなり例へば敵は何程取掛らんとする勢を示すと雖も

無我無心の位の事

一五

190

Regarding the State of Mu-Ga-Mu-Shin, [25] Without Self, Without Mind

For the most part, when your eyes fix on some part of the opponent, your Energy is focused and you employ a Kata in that moment. This happened because your mind naturally focused on a certain point. This is known as "allowing your mind to go where it pleases." Thus it all depends on what your opponent does.

For example, no matter how intense your opponent's grabs or attacks may be, you should remain as if asleep and you should not favor anything. Your mind should be perfectly clear and your spirit tranquil. In other words in a state of Mu-Ga-Mu-Shin, Without Self, Without Mind. It is essential that you use your Waza while in that state of Without Self, Without Mind. Therefore this should be your focus when training. There are many more examples of this that I will record for instructor's use.

---

[25] The words Mu-Ga-Mu-Shin, when directly translated mean "Without Self, Without Mind" however this refers to a mind that has not been distracted, lost or trapped by some worry.

The writer Sakakibara Koresuke 榊原伊祐 described it in his 1874 book, *A Gathering of Stories* 寄合ばなし as follows:

Without Self, Without Mind describes a person who is completely dedicate to their purpose, and who devotes their whole spirt to their industry without distraction.

柔　術　教　科　書

我は只眠りたるが如く敢て好まず能く心を正明に爲し泰然安座したる處の如きを以て則ち無我無心と云ふなり無我無心の所より出で敵に應じて業を行ふ事肝要なれば宜しく考へて修業すべし。是れに就ての喩言澤山あり教師用に著はす。

不動心の位の事

一六

不動心の位の事

不動心と云ふ事は即ち如何なる事に遇ふも心の動かざるを云ふなり。心正明にして總身に氣滿ち渡り眼に白刃を見るも心には見ざるが如く又耳に大砲の音を聞きても聞ざるが如く凡て物毎に驚き噪がざる心を大丈夫の不動心と云ふ。斯の如き心膽を以て我身を働かし千變萬化の術を行ひ大敵に出遇ふとも少しも驚き懼るゝ事なきを即ち眞の不動心と云ふ故に往時は生れながらにして自然大砲の響或は太刀音を聽き劍撃を以て勝負を爭ふ事の常なれば隨つて心膽の修練も出來得たるなるべし。最も其頃

How to Maintain a State of Fudoshin Immovable Mind

Fudoshin, Immovable Mind, refers to the Lord of Light Fudomyo-o, who is unwavering is his goal of enlightening non-believers to the wisdom of the Buddha, which he does by force if necessary.

A state of Fudoshin means that no matter what occurs around you, your mind does not move. In short, you remain focused and not distracted. Your mind remains clear and true and your energy permeates your entire body. Even if someone draws a sword right in front of your eyes, you remain focused and not distracted. Further, even if the sound of a cannon firing reaches your ear, the sound does not register. A strong mind that is not able to be swayed by sudden action is what is meant by Fudoshin.

If you move your body while maintaining this state of mind, you will be able to employ techniques with 1000 variations and 10,000 different combinations. You will be able to remain calm and centered even if you encounter a fierce opponent. What I am describing is true Fudoshin.

Long ago, when people felt the reverberations of cannon or heard the sound of swords being drawn, they were trained, almost from the day they were born, to naturally react by employing swordsmanship and entering a life or death duel. This was just part of everyday life and their minds were completely trained to react in that fashion.

In that era, in order to train the mind they would sleep in fields and walk through the mountains. Further, they would venture to uninhabited areas. The goal when doing this intensive training was to prevent the mind from wandering. They sought to achieve a true state of Fudoshin.

On the other hand, nowadays many people who are doing intensive training in Jujutsu only focus developing this art in their hands and feet. There is no technique in their bellies. Therefore I call on them to consider carefully what maintaining a state of Fudoshin is about, and devote themselves exclusively to developing ways of understanding and using this state of mind. This should be more than just words, since Fudoshin will enable you develop an understanding of the essence of each technique. There are other examples of this which I will include in the instructor's edition.

柔術教科書

にても膽力を練る爲め野に臥し山に入り又は人跡絶へたる處へ
行き凡て心中の動せざる事を專一に修業爲したるもの故眞に不
動心の位にも至りしと成るべし。
亦當世の修業者と云ふは多くは手足にてのみの藝にて腹の中に
は術なきが如し依って此處を能く熟考して不動心の位に至るの
工風を專一に修業すべし只々口で云ふ斗りでなく術の極意を究
むる事を考ふべし。尙ほ引言あるも敎師用に著はす。

膽力を練磨する事

凡て武術は膽力が第一なり臆病風に誘はれて勝つべき業も其效
立たず。強敵と恐るゝ時は下手の者にも貢る事云ふまでもなく
一眼二早速と云ふ喻への如くなれど膽力なき時は其働を一つも
起す心なく怖氣附けば四肢も固くなる故に膽力の強き者が必ず
勝を取ること昔より其例多し。修業中は何よりも膽力を練るを

膽力を練磨する事

一七

194

How to Develop and Refine Your Confidence and Bravery[26]

As with all martial arts Tanryoku, or Confidence and Bravery, is the most important aspect. If the winds of cowardice are blowing, then even a technique that would surely lead to victory will be ineffective. Further, if you are faced with a fierce opponent while you yourself are not particularly skilled, defeat is not necessarily inevitable. It's like the saying,

Look first, then move quickly.

If you do not have confidence you will not be able to apply a single technique. If you are fearful your limbs will become rigid, thus practitioners that are confident and brave will always achieve victory. Many examples of this can be found in the past. When you are training, developing confidence should be of paramount importance. There are many examples of sayings related to this that I will record in the instructor's manual.

---

[26] The word Tanryoku seems to be both "being unafraid" as well as "being full of spirit, or confidence."

沈着を守る事

第一とすべし。喩の引言種々あれども教師用として著はす。

一八

柔術敎科書

沈着を守る事

總じて武術の類には諺に云ふ急ては事を仕損ずると云ふ如く不動心の無我無心にて敵より仕掛け來たる時は心を靜かにして向ふべし心周章てゝ其仕掛けを外す爲めに反つて投げらるゝ事あり。四肢の働きは早業が第一なり美麗なる勝を取るものは業の妙技に依つて先んじて敵を倒しても殘心には沈着を守り又直ぐに何を仕掛けらるゝも恐るゝ心なく、我身を守り居るは是れ武術の奥深き處なり。其内にも柔術は無手無刀なる故敵より棒劍何の武器を以て打ち掛かるも沈着を守り敵の得物を捥ぎ取り或は打落すが如きは我柔道の得意とする所にして常に沈着に行動するやう心掛くべし。

How to Remain Calm

There is a saying that applies to all martial arts, *If you feel the need to rush, your application will be poor.* When an enemy attacks, you should face him calmly in a state of Mu-Ga-Mu-Shin, Without Self, Without Mind. This is the definition of Fudoshin, the Immovable Mind. If you are distracted or troubled, then the action you take to counter the enemy's attack will fail and may cause you to be thrown.

Your most important concern should be to move every part of your body rapidly in order to apply a Waza. A beautiful win can only be achieved later, after you have developed an understanding of the subtleties of Jujutsu.

Even if you topple your enemy first you must take Zanshin, Remaining Mind. Zanshin means to remain calm and unafraid as you watch to ensure your opponent does not try another attack. This way of guarding your body is an inner secret of martial arts.

Another inner secret of Jujutsu is Mute-Muto, which means fighting empty-handed against an opponent with a Katana. If an enemy strikes at you with a staff, sword or any other weapon, you are able to calmly defend yourself by wrenching the weapon away from him. You can also use that skill particular to Judo and, strike him before throwing him to the ground. You should always remain calm and centered as you move.

眼の配りの事

凡そ眼の働きは心の發動に據るものなり。故人云ひ傳へたるが如く。物を觀て其心を起すは是れ人事一般なり。人は如何なる場合害を彼るやも計り知れざるが故に平生步行するにも柔道を練習する者は前後左右に心を配り油斷無く通行するものなり。又不意を打たれて諸人の笑を受くることありては多年の稽古も其効無なり。又兩手共に五指の內親指を中に折り込み居ることを定指と云ひて必ず親指を大切にすることなり。眼の働きに依り勇氣も滿ち又業も早速に起るものにて稽古中も相手が右へ投げんとするか又は左へ投ぐるかと相手の胸中を知るは唯相手の眼の配り方にて知り得るものなれば我は其機を速に看破する樣修業すべし。

眼の配りの事

How to Place Your Eyes

Generally speaking the way your eyes move is prompted by the activation of the spirit. This is just as Sensei that have passed away taught. It is human nature for your spirit to react when it sees something.

People never know when they may encounter a dangerous situation that could lead to injury. Thus even when you are out walking on a normal day, those that train in Judo should, without fail, maintain awareness of what is in front, behind and to either side of them as they proceed. If you were caught unaware and struck, all the other people around would surely laugh at you and years of training would go up in smoke.

Further, both hands should be kept with the fingers curled around the thumb, which is called Oyayubi, or Parent Finger, in Japanese. The Parent Finger is also known as Joshi, or the deciding finger that also represents concentration. Therefore you should always guard your thumb.[27]

The movement of your eyes can reflect the how full of martial energy you are. Further, during training understanding that in his heart your opponent is going to try and throw you to the right, or he is going to try and throw you to the left, is because you have recognized it in the way he moves his eyes and what he focuses on. We must all train extensively to detect that look and react swiftly to that chance.

---

[27] This illustration from Judo: A New Instructor's Manual by Sugawara Sadamoto published in 1925 is titled "Atemi no Ken" striking fist. It shows the thumb tucked under all the fingers.

書 科 敎 術 柔

掛聲を大切とする事

劍、柔、槍、棒、長巻、凡て武藝に於ては掛聲を發する事を必要とする。

打込み、投げ、拂ひ等には(エイ)とか(ヤア)又は(トウ)と云ふ掛聲を發す

る爲に業に勢ひ生じ又美麗に見ゆるなり。

又形に於て掛聲無き流儀あるも十中の九迄は必ず掛聲あり聲を

掛くるは氣合を込めると同じ事にて受る方より(エイ)と聲を發す

る時下腹より自然に起るものなり。捕方に於ても(チー)と答を同

時に發するものなり是れ氣と氣を起して勇氣の增すものなり。

亂捕と云へども投る際は掛聲と共に業を行ふ同時に四肢の動勢

滿つると云へば常に心に込め後進者へ稽古を授くる時試るべし。

殘心放心と云ふ事

殘心と云ふは敵に投げ倒されても起き揚る迄も心に油斷なく敵

二〇

Why Kakegoe is Important

Kakegoe, a shout unifying body and spirit, are essential in Kenjutsu, Jujutsu, Sojutsu (spear-fighting,) Bojutsu (staff-fighting) and Nagamaki-jutsu (longsword fighting) and all other martial arts. When you strike, throw, sweep and so on you shout Kakegoe of *Ei! Yaa!* or *Toh!* in order to add power and vigor to your Waza. In addition, Kakego also make the techniques more beautiful to the observer.

Though some schools do not use Kakegoe, out of every ten schools, nine of them always use Kakegoe. Kakegoe means the same thing as Kiai. When the Uke shouts *Ei!* it naturally puts power in his lower abdomen. The Tori responds simultaneously with *Ooh!* The effect is the energy of one practitioner is reflected in the energy of the other and the brave martial spirit of both is increased.

When doing a throw in Randori you would shout a Kakegoe the same time you execute the Waza. This will infuse all parts of your body with that movement. This should be made a part of your everyday training and when you teach the next generation demonstrate it clearly.

柔術教科書

を見詰め居るを云ふ。放心と云ふは投げられながら投げたる者に注目しながら起き上り又更に心を起す迄の心の動かぬ處を云ふなり。都而柔術の形に於ても投げても投げられても眼と眼を他に散らさぬ樣に白眼で心に弛みなき事を殘心放心と云ふ。投ぐる方には殘心の氣を込め投げらるゝ方を放心と云ふと雖も是亦解釋すれば殘心と同意氣のものなり。又武術の殘心と云ふことは極必要の事にて稽古中にも此の殘心の方は最も充分に修業すること肝要なり。殘心がなき形は其人の勇氣心更に無きものと知るべし。

他流試合の心得の事

僅かの武術を自慢して只他流試合を試みんと思ひ我が力と藝術練習の爲めなりなぞと先を侮り仕合を申込むが如きは最も愼むべきことなり。諸學校生徒にして仕合を申込には何々學校の何

他流試合の心得の事

二二

Zanshin and Hoshin, Remaining Mind and Freed Mind

Zanshin, or Remaining Mind, refers to remaining vigilant after you have thrown or toppled your opponent. You must not allow your mind to wander, but observe him carefully until he returns to his feet.

Hoshin, or Freed Mind, is the state the person being thrown should be in. If you have been thrown, Hoshin means you should focus your attention on the person that threw you until you get back on your feet. It can also refer to maintaining that focus until you become centered again and not allowing your mind to wander.

You and your opponent should be maintaining eye contact while doing every Jujutsu Kata. Two combatants glaring at each other and not allowing their spirit to slacken during training is what is meant by Sanshin and Hoshin. The person throwing should maintain Zanshin and not allow his focus to wander, while the person being thrown should maintain Hoshin. Though these two words are different, upon close inspection they both refer to Zanshin.

I would like to conclude by saying that Zanshin is utterly essential for martial arts practice. Developing good Zanshin is a fundamental aspect of training and great care should be taken to develop this mindset. A Kata performed without Zanshin means you have no martial spirit in your heart and mind.

他流試合の心得の事

段何級の者及姓名年齢等を書き誌して仕合を行ふべし、其の時は我れ未熟なりと思はず自身の得手を相手に仕掛け見るべし必ず我が得手を先方へ知られぬ様にすべし、餘は卷中各箇條に示す。初心の内は通りを常に心得居れば少しも敵に恐るゝことなし。試合する場合には胸に動氣起り相手に業を掛くべきか掛けらるゝか怖氣を生じ易し。故に場馴れたる者は七分の徳あり、町道場などには隨分業の上手なる者にても他流試合其他大會等へ出席すると意外に早く貫くる者あり。是れ心に臆するが故なり相手は左程強くはなかりしになどゝ後にて悔んでも其詮なし。又他流試合に出づる時は相手は強きには相違ないが常に得意と自信する所の業を以て恐れずに掛け其手が外れたら又此の手と自信を以て打掛りなば決して恐るゝに足らず。然し亦敵を輕く見れば我れに油斷生じ甚だ不利なれば常に怠らず修練せば強者なりとも恐るゝに足らざるべし。

三

Regarding Dueling With Other Schools

I would like to offer a word of warning to practitioners who have developed a bit of pride in their newfound ability in martial arts and who want to try and duel with students at another school. While your goal is to test your power and develop your technique, casually applying for a Taryujiai, Duel With Another School, is something you should be extremely careful about.

When you make an application for a duel to any school,[28] you should write the name of your school and include what Dan rank or Kyu rank you are. You must also include your first and last name, your age and so forth when writing this application. When applying, do not think of yourself as unskilled, rather consider the experience a chance to test out your strongest techniques on an opponent. You should never reveal your particular skill set to the tother school in advance. The reason for this was explained in the previous chapters of this document. If you maintain an everyday state of mind when facing off against an opponent you will not be afraid in the least.

In the beginning, when you enter a duel outside your own school, it will be easy for you to become nervous and unsure about whether to attack with this Waza or that. On the other hand, those with experience in such situations will be better prepared.

When you go to a Machi-dojo, a local town Dojo, be aware that even quite skilled practitioners can be defeated quickly. This is quite surprising and happens at Taryujiai as well as large tournaments. This is because they have fear in their hearts. This is doubly lamentable if it turns out your opponent was not particularly skilled.

Also when doing a Taryujiai and your opponent is strong, accept that fact and face him without fear. Try to apply the Waza you are most adept at and, should that fail, stay confident and simply say, "Well how about this technique" and continue the match. By keeping this attitude you will not be afraid.

---

[28] Initially this was talking about dueling with a member of another school of Jujutsu, but now the "school" is referring to the Judo program at a public school or university.

稽古に相手を忌み嫌ふ事

柔術教科書

道場に稽古中相手を選むは上達せざる基なり。故に多人数中不親切なる教へ方を爲す者徃々あり斯る者と稽古を好まざるは一般の通有性なれど斯くては毎日同じ人とばかり稽古を爲し居りては業も不進可成多人數と稽古するを宜しとす。若し不親切なる者に出遇はゞ其者の得意の手の裏を考へて始終相手を破れば終には其者も好意を以て迎へ互に研究する樣になるものなり又自分より相手が弱くて自分の心の儘になると其者のみと稽古する幣徃々あり是れ卑劣なるのみならず又上達せざるなり後進の者には親切叮嚀に教へてこそ武士道の意義にも叶ふなり。又他流試合の掛引等は自然會得するものなれば相手を選むが如きは稽古中斷じて愼むべし。

二三

As a final note, underestimating your opponent can mean you are becoming careless and can lead to an unfortunate outcome. Be ever mindful of this and do not become lazy. If you continue to train with intensity you will become strong and others will become unbelievably fearful of you.

Having a Loathing For Certain Partners During Training

If you have a habit of picking your opponents at the Dojo, it will form a barrier to excelling at this art. Since there are a lot of people training, it goes without saying that you will frequently encounter some who do not teach in a friendly manner. While it might be natural to dislike training with such people, if you train with the same people every day, your Waza will not progress. It is in your best interest to train with as many different people as possible.

If you meet someone who you feel is unkind, consider a way to counter his preferred technique. In the end you will be able to defeat him and likely develop a more positive impression of him. You will then be able to research techniques together.

Another aspect of this is when your opponent is considerably weaker than you. If you only train with a person who does not pressure you in any way, your technique will not only become cowardly, but training exclusively with such a person will prevent you from becoming adept at Judo.

You should always teach the next generation in a friendly and manner, explaining the details carefully. However, your teaching method must also be consistent with the true meaning of Bushido.

Finally, when doing a Taryujiai, you will naturally become adept at using Kake-Hiki, strategy, however when it comes to selecting partners for training using strategy is absolutely forbidden.

強情は武藝の大惡と云ふ事

何事を習ふにも敎師の敎に能く隨ひ一心に學びてこそ眞上達す、るなれ身體強壯にして力量あるに慢心し木造の人形の如くに突張りなどする者は必ず其業上達せざるなり。己が身體は四肢と下腹に力を込めイザ投ぐるとか又突く引く等の場合に氣合と同時に迅速に業の妙處を現はすものなり。都而己に力量ありとも敎を受くる時は從順に熱心に練習すれば熟達疑ひなし。必強情をつゝしむべし。

稽古前後の心得

道場及自宅にて假にも稽古を爲す時は大小用便は必ずも濟ませたる後稽古に掛かること萬一假死したる時大小便を洩らす事あり。大食後大酒後は必ず稽古を爲さざること他人稽古中には極

Being Stubborn is A Great Evil in Martial Arts

No matter what you are studying, you should follow your instructor's teaching and devote yourself entirely to studying the material. This will enable you to become completely proficient.

However, if you are devoting yourself to making your body powerful and become so prideful in your strength that your body is as rigid as a wooden doll, you will never master this art.

What should happen is you put power into all your limbs as well as in your lower abdomen. Then, the instant you throw, strike or pull an opponent you should unify both your body and spirit as you rapidly apply Waza. This is the way to demonstrate the subtleties of this art.

Even though you may have great strength, when being taught, be sure to accept the instructions you are given and train with passion. By doing so there is no doubt you will become an excellent Jujutsu practitioner. However, you should always refrain from being stubborn.

柔　術　教　科　書

めて静かに見學し居る事。凡て稽古に掛かる時は立際ともに足の位置は八字型のこと。見所立ちある時は正面の所へ先に禮を爲し次に見所に向ひ一禮して其道場の中央にて雙方互に一禮して稽古に掛るべし稽古終りたる時は始めの如く見所正面に禮して引下るを儀式とす。輕々しき舉動有りて他流の人に笑ひを受けぬ樣に注意すべし。稽古終りたれば水にて能く汗を拭ひ清潔にして衣類を着用する事と心得べし。又試合及稽古の際後進者に貧くる事あるとも必ず恨む可からず又他の場所にて勝つことあり勝負は時の運と諺にもあるなり。

精神と態度の事

諸武藝には更なり就中柔術にありては沈着の態度こそ必要なれ。何となれば柔術は敵を嫌はず又敵の業に倣ひて我れ亦其の氣に合せて表裏の考へを爲すものなり是れ精神の作用なれば必ず感

二五

Things to Do Before and After Training

Even if you are only going to train for a short time at the Dojo, or your home, always be sure to urinate and defecate first. The reason is because if you are knocked out during training you may urinate or defecate on yourself. While this is unlikely, you should take precautions. Always refrain from training after you have eaten a large meal or drunk a large amount of Sake.

When doing Kengaku, or observing others training, you should be utterly silent. While training is in progress you should be standing just outside the training area, with your feet in Hachijigata, or like the Kanji for the number 8, 八.

When your match will be observed, you should first bow to the front of the Dojo, then bow to the observer. The two practitioners move to the center of the Dojo, and bow to each other before beginning training. After training the process should repeat what you did initially, bowing first to the observer and then to the front of the Dojo before withdrawing. This is the proper etiquette.

You should be careful that you do not behave in a caviler manner unless you want to invite the laughter of other schools.
After you finish training, wet a cloth with water and wipe all the sweat off your body until you are clean. You should then put on clothes.

As a final note, if during training or a match, you are defeated by a younger practitioner you should never become resentful. You will invariably win at another time or place. There is a saying *you win some, you lose some.*

柔術教科書

ずる處ありて初めて面に現はれると云ふ無形のものなり其無形
物より有形の働きを神態度となる此態度こそ活動の第一指針に
して禮に初まり禮に終るものなれば修業者は沈着にして最も謹
みて事に當るべし。次に解く處を能く熟讀すべし。

精神――執意

禮義
信情
忠孝
喜怒
愁悲

禮の解

禮は精神の解釋中最も解し難きものにして禮は精神より出て態
度に顯るゝを云ふ、然れば此の心の禮なき時は貴顯に對し亦神靈

Spirit and Attitude

It is essential that you remain calm during Jujutsu training. While this applies to any martial art it is particularly necessary for Jujutsu. The reason is Jujutsu practitioners do not hate their enemy rather they hope to learn the Waza used by the enemy and try and match their opponent's spirit. A Jujutsu practitioner is always thinking of Hyori, meaning both sides of the duel.

Since training is the application of your Seishin, or mental energy, you will always be able to sense something in your opponent. Though you will first become aware of it on his face, it is something shapeless. However, that shapeless thing causes a real response which is a divine attitude.

That attitude is the primary guiding principle and is why we begin with a bow and end with a bow. Thus, those doing intensive training should be careful about remaining calm and focused. The next section will explain many terms so be sure to read carefully.

Spirit				
Adhering to a State of Mind				
Fear	Joy	Honor	Belief	Respect
Sadness	Anger	Fealty	Emotion	Justice

柔　術　教　科　書

に對する柔の術の投合する心より出でたる容姿は迎も出來ざるものと心得べき事。

義の解

義は最も柔術中十中の八九迄も伴はざるはなし義に就きて解釋すればなかく限り無きものなれども是は柔術の性質として離るべからざるものなれば熟達と伴ふて自然其意の備ふるにより未熟の中は業に無理あり即ち無法の仕向を敵に仕掛けざる樣注意するが肝要なり。

信の解

信の意に就きて二つあり事武藝及術の意に投合する樣自得に勤むると云ひ次に信を以てする容姿は如何のものであると云ふことを心掛れば足れりと知るべし。

義の解、信の解

二七

An Explanation of Rei, Respect

Explaining how respect relates to the mind and spirit is extremely difficult. Respect is the attitude that emanates from your spirit. However, if you do not have respect in your heart you will not be able to unify the two parts that make up Jujutsu: soft and flexible combined with technique. Understand that if you cannot do this, you will not be able to present yourself properly when in front of a distinguished person or a divine spirit.[29]

An Explanation of Gi, Justice/Doctrine

For the most part questions of Justice to not appear in Jujutsu, perhaps out of 10 situations, 8 or 9 will have nothing to do with it. If I were to start talking about what is meant by Justice I am afraid I might never finish, however Justice cannot be separated from the fabric that makes up Jujutsu.

As a practitioner becomes experienced, he naturally develops an understanding of this this subject. However, this concept is quite difficult for inexperienced practitioners to grasp. For those practitioners, it is essential that you explain to them the importance of not trying some illegal trick on their opponent.

The Meaning of Shin, Belief

There are two meanings for Shin, Belief. One is the action of trying to develop an understanding of the unity of martial arts and technique. The second is contemplating what such a unification should look like. The act of contemplating this is enough.

---

[29] "Divine Spirit" may be referring to the Emperor of Japan.

柔 術 教 科 書

情 の 解

情は就中甲者に乙者とに關係深きものなるが故に情は愁と悲み との似て否なるものを區別し判斷力を備ふるにて足れるなり。

忠孝 の 解

君に忠親に仕へて孝は其の區別を辨へる事唯形斗りとならざる 樣注意すれば足れりとす。

喜 の 解

喜とは勝ちたるときに笑顔を現はすが如きをば云ふ。喜あれば 色面に現はるゝは是れ人の常なり勝擧を愼むべきこととなり。

怒 の 解

The Meaning of Jo, Emotion

Above all Emotion refers to the relationship between the person doing the technique and the person receiving the technique. Thus while emotion does contain worry and sadness you need to have the ability to separate those aspects.

The Meaning of Chuko, Fealty and Loyalty

There is loyalty to your lord and loyalty to your parents. If you are able to discern that there is more to this than two separate categories and are able to consider that fact, it will be enough.

The Meaning of Yorokobi, Joy

Yorokobi, or Joy, is what appears on your face after you are victorious. It is quite natural for your face to change color when you are overjoyed. However, you should always exercise prudence when in the thrill of victory.

柔　術　教　科　書

怒りと云ふは是物に觸れて心に反動を起すを云ふなり業の意に依れば概ね無念の怒なるが故に其心を戒しめ業を學ぶべし決して荒々敷怒氣を面に顯はすは不可なり何となれば怒らずとも鋭き眼にて其場に臨めば怒は充分に現はれるものなればなり。

愁の解

愁は憂ふことの面の牛ば顯れたるものにて悲と又同ふせざる事を注意すべし。貢るとも愁ふること勿れ。

悲の解

悲は憂事の最早全部をば面に顯したるもの愁悲此の二つの區別を解して精神活動の道理を自得すべし。此以上は單に柔術の精神を述べたるに過ぎされば詳精は圖解に依りて會得せらるべし。

怒の解、悲の解

二九

The Meaning of Ikari, Anger

Anger appears when you interact with something that causes a response in your mind. As it relates to Waza, anger is usually something you regret. Thus, you need to discipline your mind when studying Waza in order to prevent wild, uncontrolled angry energy from appearing on your face. Though you need to put an intense sharpness to your eyes, it should be without anger. When you are actually in an intense situation your anger will surely manifest itself.

The Meaning of Urei, Worry

To worry means the same thing as to be anxious. If you are worried it will appear on your face. However, you should be careful not to confuse this with sadness, which is not the same thing. You should not worry about being defeated.

The Meaning of Kanashimi, Sadness

Sadness comes from a bitter experience, and is immediately apparent all over your face. You should consider how Worry is different from Sadness and keep them separate in your mind as you develop an understanding of the principles of how your mind and spirit operate.

This ends the section giving a simple overview of Jujutsu Seishin, the mental aspects of Jujutsu. You will be able to develop a greater understanding of this in the illustrated descriptions later in this book.

柔術敎科書

陰陽強弱之説及一身の心を論ずる事

夫敵には陰敵と陽敵二とありて其容姿にては判じ難きものあり外見弱き風情にても其實剛敵なるものあり又外見勢ひ盛んにして強氣に見へても其實却つて弱き者あり。柔術の法は一身を靜かにして變化を常とすれば一樣に云ひ難しと雖も仕合に臨みて敵の面に注目し能く其色を見てなすべし。

又敵の顏色赤くなるは性氣上りたるものなり性氣發すれば必ず心に急く爲めに勝利を得る工風するの暇なし又顏色靑白くなる者は心に臆したると知るべし。臆する時は身體震ふ爲めに業の活用出來ざるなり。他流試合の第一の心得は臆せざるにあり。

わが上に立つ藝術を苦にやむな好きの道こそ上達なるべし

八方へくばる眼のすき間なき

古歌

An Explanation of Yin and Yang as well as Strong and Weak
Additional: A Discussion of the Whole Mind

There are two types of opponents Yin opponents and Yang opponents, however distinguishing between the two is difficult. For example a person can appear weak and unassuming on the outside however he can turn out to be a ferocious opponent. On the other hand, the opponent may seem to be bustling with energy and confidence yet turn out to be a weak opponent.

The way the Jujutsu method works requires you to completely relax your body and prepare for any eventuality. It is hard to put in words, however during a bout you should watch the color of the opponent's face.

If your opponent's face is red that means his energy is flowing. When a person becomes excited his heartrate will increase and he will not have a chance to develop a strategy for winning. On the other hand a person whose face has gone pale means they have a cowardly spirit. When frightened your body will shake, meaning you will be unable to apply a Waza. The most important thing when doing a Taryujiai is to clear away any timidity.

Do not agonize over the martial artists who are above you in skill
Follow the road you like and you will develop great skill

An old poem

Your eyes should cover what is happening in all eight directions
around you
Your vigilance leaves no gap for disaster to slip through

The Author

柔　術　教　科　書

心
魂
｜
心

┌──────┴──────┐
膽　　　　　動
力　　　　　勢

作　身　　修
業　體　　身
呼　の　　練
吸　發　　習
　　育

心の割出五系の圖解の事

身に禍のきたるひまなし

著者

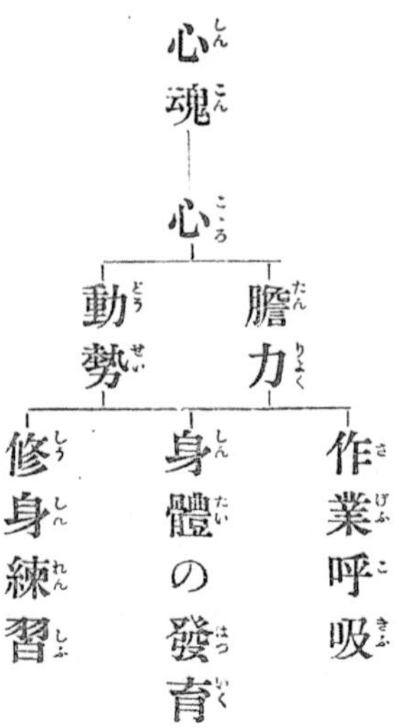

心魂とは人の心が基にて萬物に當りて皆觀るものにて其心が起るものなり是れ第一の魂の基なり。種々に割出し強きにも弱きにも力むも勢も出づるなり此れを詳細に解説すれば限りなきものなれど五種に心の働きを曰ひ顯せば心より動勢である。仕合する時に當り敵を見る時は勝と云ふ心を起して勢滿るものなり

心の割出五系の圖解の事

三一

An Illustrated Chart of the Five Elements of the Mind

Shinkon, the heart and soul, forms the basis of a person's mind. It interacts with all things and allows you to observe them causing a reaction in your mind. This is the first part of what forms the soul. We can break this down even further, into the following: strength, weakness, power and vigor.

If I tried to explain all of these in detail the explanation would go on forever, however there are five basic operations of the spirit. The first of these is Dosei, Movement. When you are set to begin a match and see your opponent, the desire to win wells up in your spirit. You become full of a vigorous energy. This is a fundamental element of the mind.

Heart and Soul		
Mind		
Movement		Courage and Grit
Training for the Entire Body and Mind	Development of the Body	Working Reseparation

ERIC SHAHAN シャハン・エリック

柔　術　教　科　書

心の割出五系の圖解の事

是れ心の基なり。

次は膽力にして勝心にならんと思ふ心起きたれば必ず心に力を起すなるべし。是は身體が基なり身體虚弱なれば其心を起すも其効なし身體を強健と爲し物に動ぜざるを以て基なりとす、次に著す處の體育法に依り幼年より此術を學び身體の消化を附けて次第に稽古を爲さば必ず自得すべし。

次第に學ぶべし、次に作業呼吸である是れ皆心より起りて自然業なり何人に教授しても教ふる方は十中の七八度迄は投げられる様にてはならず前に逃べたるが如く身體を練へ置くこと肝要の形を造り人に教へ得るは云ふまでもなし。又武術は息切れす

體育法に心掛くるが肝要なり。試合に臨み息切せざらんとするには幼年より中年にて修業する人を見ても知れるものなり業は早く覺ゆるも息切れして長く續かぬものなり。

又次に修身の解我が身體弱きときは到底上手名人には爲れぬも

三二

224

The next is Tanryoku, Courage and Grit. When you have become determined to win, it is because your mind has been activated. Once activated your mind causes power to become activated. Power is what your body uses to act.

However, if your body is feeble even if your mind becomes activated it will be to no avail. You must make your body strong and healthy, which is a fundamental as it allows you to not be moved by things. The next part of developing courage and grit is the physical education method you use. If you study this art from a young age and absorb its lessons into your body, the continued training will enable you to naturally develop courage and grit. You will see this as you follow the progression of illustrated lessons in this book.

The next topic is Sagyou Kokyu, Working Respiration. This originates in everyone's mind and naturally increases or decreases along with the Waza you are doing. There is no need to teach people how to do this. However, you should never become winded during martial arts training, which is why I previously talked about how forging the body is essential.

As anyone who teaches can tell you the person being taught will be thrown 7 or 8 times out of 10. The only way to avoid getting out of breath during a tournament is to begin this training method from a very young age. This is essential. If you look at middle-aged Jujutsu practitioners you can see they are in shape. Even if you are able to learn Waza quickly, shortness of breath will mean you cannot continue for a long time.

柔 術 教 科 書

のなれば常に讀書を怠らず智德を進むるは云ふまでもなく能く
理非を辨へ仁義を明らかにしてこそ名人上手にも成り得るべけ
れば絶えず稽古を勵み術を練磨するが肝要なり、いつに至るも他
人に敎へを受け居るは愚の至りなり後進を引立て自身の業を磨
くが心の基なり。

道場及勝負見所の事

凡武德會又は講道館等廣大なる道場を始めとし各學校町道場の
定法として支闘より右に見所を置定なり。
武術は都て仕合の時
は審判官見所が四角に立ち行事もありて其行事は唯業の美事に
勝を得る者を指して美事とか勝負ありとか角力の行事と同じ役
を務め行事見所より檢査する者なり。
勝負には見
苦き勝を取たる時は六分或は七分として全くの勝に入れず。
再び何分かの勝を得たる時前のと合て一本の勝を得るなり。
大

三三

Next I would like to discuss Shintai no Hatsuiku, Development of the Body. This goes without saying but, if your body is weak there is no way for you to become famous as a skilled practitioner. However, by the same token, if you do not make a habit of reading your knowledge and virtue will not develop.

Having a clear understanding of right and wrong, humanity and justice is essential to becoming a famous and skilled practitioner. That being said, it is essential that you must devote yourself to training without ceasing in order to forge and polish your technique. Eventually this will lead to you becoming a person who teaches others. Thus, in order to enable the next generation, you need to set your mind to polishing your technique.

柔　術　教　科　書

概は三本勝負の事故雙方一本宛勝を取れば後一本にて勝負が附くなり此場合行事は「勝負」と大聲を發して試合者に注意を與ふるなり。五分の勝負の時は引分になること相撲の三番勝負と略同じことなり。修業者は見所の立ち居る時は特に勝敗とも美麗になすこと苦しき試合を爲して諸人の笑ひを受けぬ樣すべし。見所より今一本と聲の掛りし時は更に勝負を爲すべし普通の場に臨む時にも禮儀を正しく爲す事は前に充分述べたる通りなれども斯る公會の演武場にては一層注意して教師及學校の名を辱しめぬ樣注意すべし。是が肝要なり

體育より柔術に進むの心得

凡體育と云ふは近來各學校にて盛んに奬勵しつゝあるも柔術を學ぶ者は幼年の頃より卷中に示す圖解の如く順を追ふて身體四肢の働き輕快にし次第に筋骨の、自由發育を進めて投ぐる、投げら

Things to Understand About the Dojo and Judging Matches

The etiquette for entering a Dojo is the same whether you are entering large Dojo like the Butokukai and the Kodokan, or smaller facilities like a school Dojo or a community Dojo. When you enter the front door the area for observing is always located to the right. For all martial arts competitions, the judges stand in one of the four official observation points at the corners of the training area and make decisions. What they decide is, simple, whether or not one practitioner used a beautiful application of Waza in order to win.

The deciding factor, "A beautiful application of Waza" is similar to how Sumo competitions are judged. If one of the officials misjudges the competitors, the officials standing in the other corners would gather and confer. If a competitor wins in an undignified manner and the judges deem the technique only 60 ~70% accurate, the match will be declared no-victory. After the match is re-started, if another victory is achieved it will be added into the previous score until, Ippon, one victory is achieved.

For the most part duels are Sanbon Shobu, or the three match system. For example, if each competitor has Ippon, one victory, then the next person to get Ippon would be the winner. The moment the competitor gets Ippon, a judge would shout Shobu!, victory and defeat has been decided! This is to get the attention of the competitors. If the duel remains 50/50 then it is handled the same way as Sanban Shobu in Sumo.

When trainees are standing in the observation area, be sure there is a clear, beautiful distinction between the winner and the loser and absolutely do not allow your bout to become a painful to watch event. This could lead to laughter and scorn.

If a judge shouts Ippon, One Victory, you still continue the bout. When taking part in a typical tournament, you should use correct manners and strictly observe all protocol. While this was all mentioned previously, when attending a tournament, redouble your commitment to observing etiquette in order to not sully the name of your instructor or school. This is an essential point to observe.

柔術教科書

る、返り身、打込み、受霞突掛、前返り、後返り、逆立、高飛等の稽古を充分に練習して後ち眞の位を自得し以て柔術に進むを眞の稽古と云ふ。凡そ何の藝道にても順を追ふて次第に業の妙を得るは已に讀者も知らるゝ處なり。此の卷中十中八位迄圖解にて著はせるも他は圖畫筆に任せぬ處ありて委しく說明出來ざりしは著者の最も遺憾とする處なり。後日敎師用として補ふ處なればそれ迄は本書にある處を勉強し給へかし。術の術極意口傳秘傳と云ふ事は斯る小册子なれども侮るべからず柔術は武術中最も高尙なるものなり。

體育より柔術に進むの心得

三五

230

Why Jujutsu is the Natural Progression from Basic Physical Fitness

Recently, schools all across Japan have been implementing physical education programs, which is quite laudable. Students that have begun Jujutsu training at a young age are able to develop skills like the ones illustrated in this manual. They have conditioned their core and limbs to move both deftly and quickly. Their muscles and bones have developed so they can move freely in any direction. Their extensive training means that they can throw, be thrown, roll, punch, receive, strike to Kasumi (the temple,) strike, flip forward, flip back, walk on their hands and jump over high objects.

When students have learned Shin no Kurai, True Stance, or the basic way to position their body, real Jujutsu training will begin in earnest. As I am sure my readers are already aware, no matter what art you choose to peruse, skills are learned in order. As you progress through the stages you move ever closer to developing an understanding of the subtle beauty of a technique, which allows you to apply it deftly.

In this scroll I will introduce 8 of the 10 stances with illustrated explanations, however the rest cannot be explained with illustrations and words brushed on paper.

In the future I plan on publishing an instructor's guide to supplement training, however for the time being I offer this book to help your learning.

Clearly the essence of Jujutsu, all the Kuden and secret esoteric teachings of Jujutsu cannot be contained in a single slim volume, however I am in no way attempting to make light of Jujutsu, which rests atop the pinnacle of all martial arts.

Training Uniform
Old-Style Training Uniform

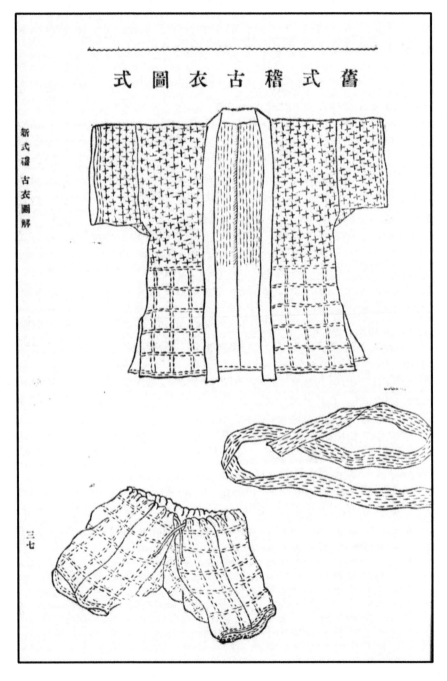

New-Style Training Uniform

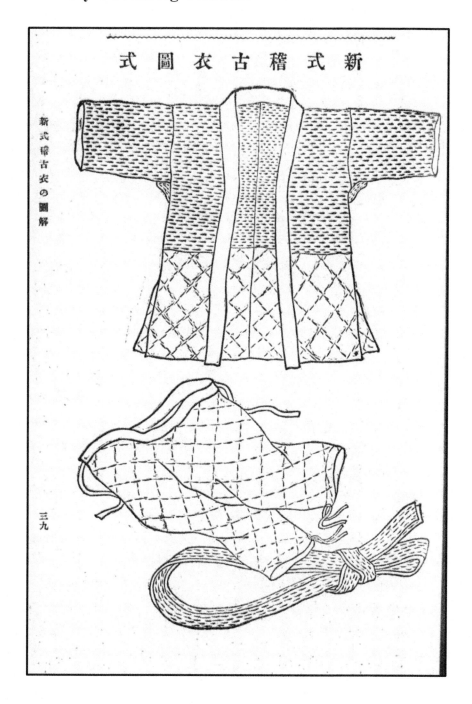

柔　術　教　科　書

舊式稽古衣の圖解

凡そ稽古衣と云ふ者は舊來より圖式の通りにて肩より腰迄を晒木綿の白地に紺糸を以てし肩袖は十字絞りに縫ひ上げ腰より下は格子形に二筋に縫ふ圖の如し。袖は半袖にて襟は丸巾の晒木綿を以て四つ折にし紺地にて縫ふこともあり。畢套又は三味又猿股は二重合せにて上部は紐を通し半股引の如く腰にて紐を締め帶は木綿の半巾を縱に四つ折とし縫ひ合はす。今回著はしだるは四肢の働きを縫方は木地に依りて白、黑糸を以て刺すなり段級の違ひ又は敎師の夫々規則を定めて造るなり。委しく見せる爲め舊式の着衣の姿を模型として寫生したり。

三六

新式稽古衣圖解

元來我國の風俗は一般に角袖なりしも近時は外國との間交通頻

Kyushiki Keikoi
Old Style Training Uniform

Most of the training uniforms you see today are the old-style, like in the illustration on the left. The top, from the shoulders to the waist, is made of white bleached cotton. The shoulders and sleeves are sewn with overlapping crosses using navy blue thread.

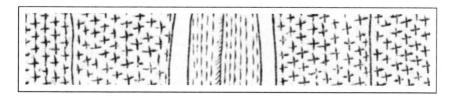

Stitching with a lattice-work pattern is done from the waist down to the hem. The lines are made with two rows of stiches.

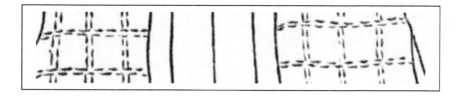

The sleeves are short. For the collar take a piece of white, untrimmed cotton cloth and fold it over 4 times and then cover it with a piece of navy blue cloth. Use white cotton thread to sew it together.

The shorts are known by several names including Kinkakushi, testicle covering, Sanmi, inner-secret, or Saru-mata, monkey pants. They are doubled and a piece of string is passed between them at the waist, making them a kind of half-pants. You tie these off at the waist.

To make the belt you tie about your waist, get a half-piece of cloth (18 centimeters in width) and fold it lengthwise 4 times then sew it together. The way you sew it depends on the material. White or black thread can be used. This also can depend on your Dankyu, rank, or the regulations given by your instructor.

The intent behind the old style uniform, which is shown on the left, was to make it easier to see the movements in the arms and legs.

柔術教科書

新式稽古衣圖解

繁となり隨て世人の服裝も多くは洋服となりたるに就て我が柔
道稽古衣も是れに倣らはざるべからず。
凡即ち袖短かく且袖口廣き我國在來の服裝にて稽古に馴れては
洋服の敵に出遇たる時勝手惡しく大に不利なれば平常より是れ
に稽古するが得策なると又近年外人間に柔術を學ぶ者年々增
加せるにより可成裸體の大部分を現はさぬ爲に改良せるなり。
又則ち袖も長く筒袖にて袖口細く畧隱しも長く白地に紺糸を以
て橫目に圖の如く刺し上下共に長くしたるなり。八つ口の處は
少し足し切を以て縫ふなり。
是舊來のに比し唯丈の長きと橫に刺したるだけにて帶は從來の
通りなり。〔黑〕は有段者〔茶〕は一、二級三四級は〔靑〕等に區別せるは從
前の通り各道場の規定に據る。
又股引は膝下二三寸の處にて紐を締めるなれども稽古の時は結
ばざるも可なり。

三八

Shinshiki Keikoi
New Style Training Uniform

Historically, the clothing worn in Japan has open sleeves however recently interactions with foreign people is increasing. At the same time there has been a shift amongst the populist towards western style clothing, therefore it is necessary for the Judo[30] uniform to adapt to this change.

If we continue to train while wearing the old style uniform, with its short, wide sleeves but then encounter an adversary wearing western clothing, we will be at a disadvantage. The only solution to eliminate this disadvantage is to train using the new style training uniform.

In addition, the number of foreigners interested in Jujutsu training has been increasing year after year. To accommodate them the training uniform has been altered to reduce the amount of exposed skin.[31]

Thus the sleeves have been extended and made more tube shaped while the opening has been narrowed. The Kinkakushi, family-jewels cover, has been made longer. The material is white cotton with horizontal stitching using navy blue thread. This can be seen in the illustration.

Both the top and bottom of the training uniform are longer than before. The opening at the armpit has been extended and sewn shut. The main difference between the new and old style are the overall extension of the arms and legs along with horizontal stitching. The belt is the same as before. Generally the colors are : black for Yudansha, brown is for 1,2 Kyu and 3,4 Kyu are blue.

These divisions vary depending on the rules of the Dojo. The shorts should extend about 2 ~ 3 Sun, 6 ~ 9 centimeters, below the knee. They are normally secured about the waist with a string, however during training some people don't tie them off.

---

[30] The author switches from Jujutsu to Judo here.

[31] Literally "to reduce the amount of nakedness."

Kamae: Stances
Jujutsu Shin no Kurai #1
True Stance #1

Stand straight with you mind free of thoughts. This is True Stance #1.

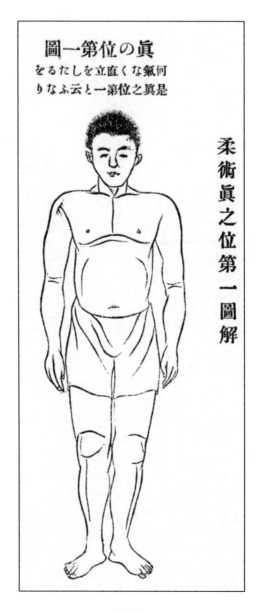

Jujutsu Shin no Kurai #2
True Stance #2

Force all your power from your shoulders down below your navel.

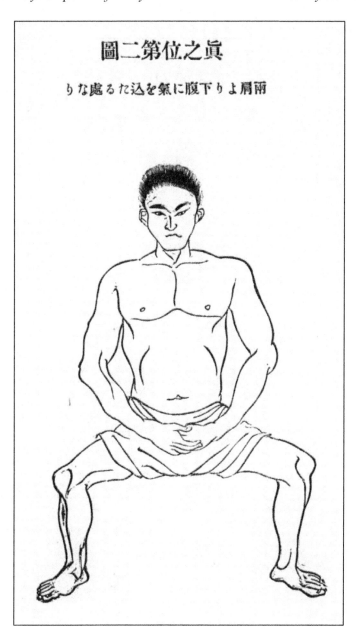

圖二第位之眞

兩肩より下腹に氣を込んだる處なり

Jujutsu Shin no Kurai #3
True Stance #3

This is how to sit in Shin no Kurai. Face straight ahead and do not allow any tension in your shoulders.

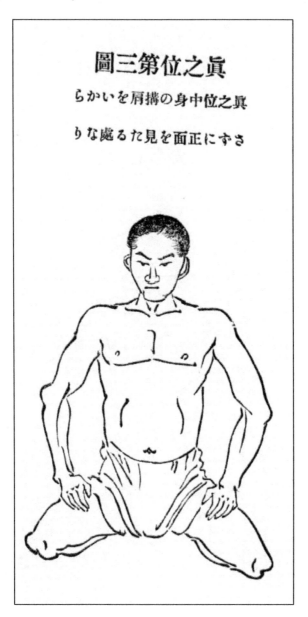

Jujutsu Shin no Kurai #4
True Stance #4

This stance is as described in the text. A stance used in training by the person executing the technique. The proper positioning is shown in the illustration. It is known colloquially as Yoko Ichimonji, Straight Line to the Side.

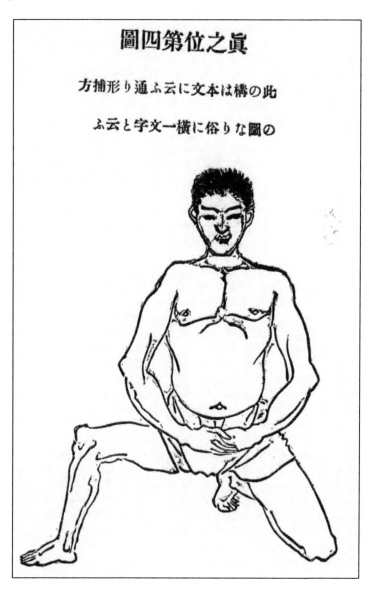

241

Jujutsu Shin no Kurai #5
True Stance #5

This stance is used when facing off against the person doing the technique during Kata training.

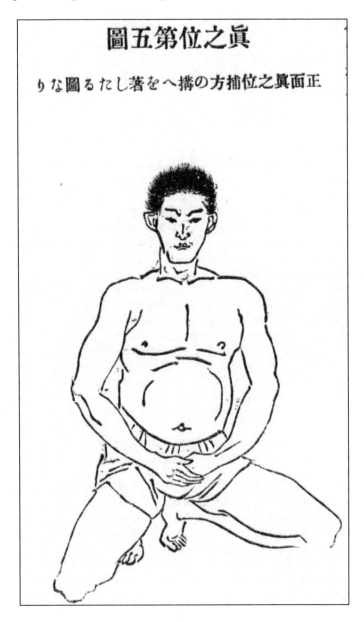

圖五第位之眞

り な 圖 る た し 著 を へ 搆 の 方 捕 位 之 眞 面 正

Overview of the 5 Shin no Kurai "True Stance" Kamae		
1	2	3

4	5

Explanation of Stances
Jujutsu Shin no Kurai
An Illustrated Explanation of Shin no Kurai #1

總て柔術は眞之位が第一の心得なり。凡武術斗りでなく總身を

働かす業をなすものは眞之位取と云ふが大事なり。

此の圖は第一直立眞之位にして變化は種々あれども眞之位と云ふ事は身體傾かず中心の崩れぬ樣下腹に力を入れて口を結び無念無想に立つを眞之位取と云ふ腹中に亂れあるときは臍下の氣息抜ける故倒れ易きものなり。

此圖五種は初心者に能く解かる樣裸體を以て見せたり。

又眞之位に付此位六ケ敷事はないのです總身に力身を込ると又身體堅くなり氣が滿る又位張と云次第にて前に云ふ無我無心と云ふ心を持て氣を鎮着てする事大肝要なり。

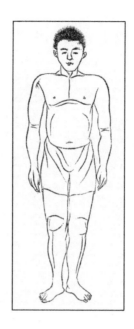

Jujutsu Shin no Kurai
An Illustrated Explanation of Shin no Kurai #1

Every technique in Jujutsu is based on Shin no Kurai, True Stance. This applies not only to the martial arts world but Shin no Kurai is important to any activity using the whole body.

This illustration shows Shin no Kurai #1. There are many variations of this stance however basically Shin no Kurai describes a stance where the body is not leaning and you core is not off balance. You have power in your lower abdomen with your mouth closed tight. The feeling of standing in Shin no Kurai is Mu-Nen-Mu-So, or Free From Worldly Thoughts. If your spirit becomes jumbled, you will forget to focus your breathing in your lower abdomen and become more likely to fall.

To make these 5 Shin no Kurai illustrations easy to understand for beginners, they are shown naked.

The Shin no Kurai stance is not particularly difficult, however you must focus your strength and stand with the feeling that your whole body is rigid with power. As was previously mentioned, you should project calmness as described in the phrase Mu-Ga-Mu-Shin, Without Self and Free From Obstructing Thoughts.

Jujutsu Shin no Kurai
An Illustrated Explanation of Shin no Kurai #2

同第二圖解

眞之位の中身と云ふて正面を白眼兩手にて陰嚢を圖の如く圍み
兩足は橫一文字に開き爪先及下腹に力を罩め腰を少しく下げて
總身に氣息充分滿ちたる處を云ふなり。

眞之位取五種とも總て形の基本なれば充分に會得すべし變化自
在の構へにて第一より順次を追て卷中にも眞之位第何圖と云事
あり故に此の定式法を能く心得るべし。

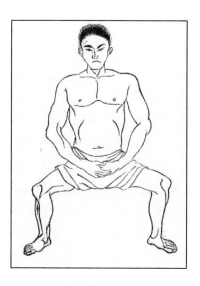

Shin no Kurai
An Illustrated Explanation of Shin no Kurai #2

Shin no Kurai #2 is known as the core stance. You are facing your opponent, glaring fiercely with both hands covering your "secret bag" or groin. Your feet are apart in Yoko Ichi Monji, or spread out with an imaginary line like the Kanji for one 1 一 . Lower your hips slightly and put power in your lower abdomen as well as your toes. This is shown in the illustration. Your breathing should energize your entire body.

The five Shin no Kurai stances form the foundation of all the Kata, so it is important to learn them all.

This stance offers complete freedom of movement, which means you can adapt to changing circumstances. You should learn all the Shin no Kurai stances, beginning with the first. As you proceed through this book, the instructions will indicate which of the five Shin no Kurai stances to adopt, thus you should pay special attention to how these prescribed forms are done.

Jujutsu Shin no Kurai
An Illustrated Explanation of Shin no Kurai #3

同第三圖解

眞之位平座の圖なり此の構へは正面を白眼て體を眞直にし下腹

に力を罩め兩膝を開きて座し兩肩を下げ兩手を股の處へ載せ口を結びて總身に氣息を滿たし中心の崩れぬ樣に爲すべきものなり。

都而柔術手合形及亂捕の稽古を爲すに當り位取の心弱ければ隨而業も速かならざるものなり。最も此中眞之位に附ては受方の構へ敵に投られるも投倒すも殘心附る迄の種々の解説あり其内にも形捕にはこの構へを以て居捕の時は大事の構へなり教師用の著書に充分なる解説をなす。

248

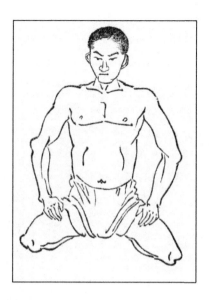

Jujutsu Shin no Kurai
An Illustrated Explanation of Shin no Kurai #3

This illustration shows Shin no Kurai #3, also known as Heiza, Seated Wide. You are seated upright and facing forward with an intense glare. You put power in your lower abdomen and sit with your legs spread. Allow your arms to hang loosely. And place your hands on your thighs. Keep your mouth closed tightly and your breathing should energize your body. Be sure your core remains stable.

This stance is used in Jujutsu competitions as well as when you do Randori training. If you are not positioned with confidence you will not be able to execute techniques quickly. There are many details regarding this stance. For example, it is primarily used by the Uke, or the person receiving the technique, or after you are thrown by the enemy. In addition, if you are thrown down, you will take this stance while maintaining Zanzhin, or maintaining a state of readiness after either victory or defeat in a duel. There are many other instructions regarding this stance including how important it is when drilling seated techniques. The instructor's manual I am writing will contain more detailed information on this.

Jujutsu Shin no Kurai
An Illustrated Explanation of Shin no Kurai #4

同第四圖解

此の形は平一文字と云ふて左膝を突きて踵を肛門の處へ當て右足を開きて爪先及下腹に力を罩め正面を見て兩手は陰嚢を圍むを平一文字と云ふ。

柔術の形捕の切は必も捕方構へにて敵に向ひ進出るも又敵を投て殘心を附るも此構への大事なる事をしれ。

250

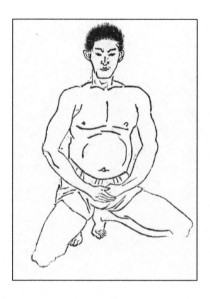

Jujutsu Shin no Kurai
An Illustrated Explanation of Shin no Kurai #4

This stance is known as Hira Ichimonji, or Wide Like the Kanji for One. Your left knee is on the ground with the heel of that foot pressing on your anus. Your right leg is upright out to the side. You should put power in your lower abdomen as well as the toes of your feet. You are facing straight ahead with both hands protecting your "secret bag" or groin. This is Hira Ichimonji.

When training Kata, you will always take this stance and advance on your opponent. It is important to remember you will also take this stance after you throw an opponent and are in Zanshin, or maintaining a state of readiness after either victory or defeat in a duel.

Jujutsu Shin no Kurai
An Illustrated Explanation of Shin no Kurai #5

同第五圖解

此の圖は平の搆へといふ。第一圖の位取に兩膝を開きて地に突

き兩足とも爪立ち身體を眞直にし、下腹に力を入れ正面を白眼で

兩手は陰嚢を圍むことおなじ圖の如し。

此も形の捕方の搆へにて右膝頭を疊に附て左り踵にて肛門の處

へ當る又亂捕に立上り前には一時は此搆へより崩れて捕に掛る

者としれ。

252

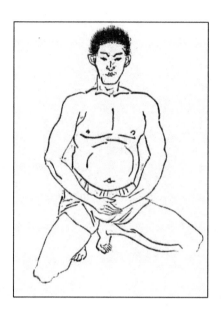

Jujutsu Shin no Kurai
An Illustrated Explanation of Shin no Kurai #5

This illustration shows the stance known as Hira, Open Wide. The illustration shows how to take this stance. Your knees are on the ground spread apart. Just your toes should be on the ground with your heels up. Your body should be straight with power in your lower abdomen. Stare straight forward with a fierce glare in your eyes. Your hands should be protecting your groin. This is shown in the illustration.

When using this stance to practice Kata, your right knee should be on the Tatami mat while your left heel is pressed near your anus. In addition, while most practitioners will stand up from this stance before beginning Randori, some practitioners will launch out of this stance and begin attacking.

Warm-up Exercises
Physical Education Exercise Step #1 : Illustrated Explanation

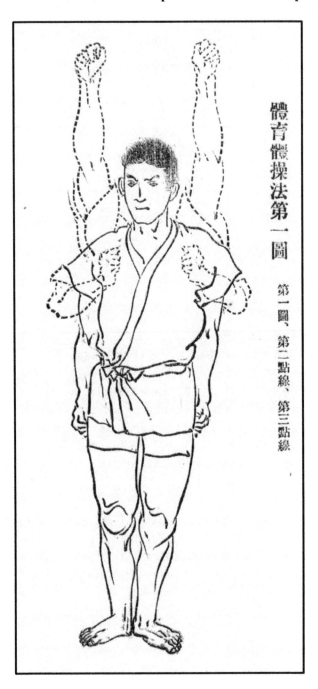

Physical Education Exercise Step #1 : Illustrated Explanation

體育體操法第一圖解

凡體操は少年の頃より諸學校にて教を受けたるものと大差なし。

此法を別に教授する處あれど獨學法にても本書に依り何人にも出來得る樣書綴あるなり。

先づ他人と學ぶ者ある時は其道場又は自宅にても直立して兩手を充分に左右へ開き指先を延して一間四方を自分一人の操練場と定め教師ある時は教授法を以て指揮するものなり。獨學する時には第一に口を結びて下腹に力をこめ眞の位第一圖の構へより爲して順次に習ふなり。

口を結ぶ時に睡吐を呑込で力を總身に入れる同時に兩手を握り

第一に頭上へ體に手を附けて押上る事點線の如くなり。

第二には兩乳の上の處へ押當兩手を第三にて元へ戻すなり。

回繰り返し次に移るなり。數

Physical Education Exercise Step #1 : Illustrated Explanation

For the most part children and youths have been taught exercise at the various schools they attend, so there is no great difference in their level of fitness. This is a separate type of instruction however this book was intended as a self-study guide, and is laid out as such, so anyone can make use of it.

First of all, if you will be learning on your own then stand straight up in the center of the Dojo or room of your house you train in. Next, stretch your arms out to the left and right and extend the tips of your fingers. To exercise you need about 1 Ken, 180 centimeters, of space on each side as well as front and back. If you have a teacher then he will have a teaching method so you should follow his instructions. When training alone, the first thing you should do is to pull your mouth tightly shut, focus your power in your lower abdomen. Then take Shin no Kurai, True Stance #1, and proceed through the lessons in this course.

When your mouth is closed, swallow your spit and force power into your entire body. At the same time close both hands into fists. Step 1 is to raise both hands above your body. This is shown with the dotted lines.

Step 2 is to bring your fists down so they are just above your nipples, then push them down so they return to the starting position.

Repeat this several times before moving on to the next exercise.

Physical Education Exercise Step #1 : Illustrated Explanation

This is a combined illustration.
 Illustration 1 is the hands at your sides (This is Shin no Kurai, True Stance #1
 Illustration 2 is your arms stretched overhead. This is shown with dotted lines.
 Illustration 3 is your fists above your nipples. This is shown with dotted lines.

Physical Education Exercise Step #2 : Illustrated Explanation

The dotted lines show how the hands press together as you arch backwards.

Physical Education Exercise Step #2 : Illustrated Explanation

體育體操法第二圖解

直立は眞の位第一圖と同じ事にして前條を終りて直に又兩足は八字形の位置となり左足より一尺五六寸も横へ開きて掌を充分に押延ばして裏表揃へて數回爲し后兩手を合して點線の如くに反り返る事圖の如し。成るべく反り返へれる丈返るべし。馴るる迄は苦しき故最初は三四回を以て壹度とし然して次へ續ける

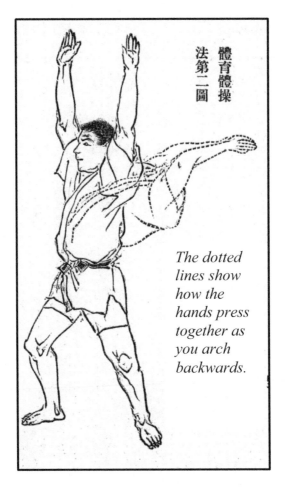

體育體操
法第二圖

The dotted lines show how the hands press together as you arch backwards.

Physical Education Exercise Step #2 : Illustrated Explanation

Start out standing straight as shown in Shin no Kurai, True Stance #1. Having finished the previous exercise, your feet will be in Hachimoji, or open like the bottom of the Kanji for 8.

Immediately step out to the side 1 Shaku and 5 or 6 Sun, 45 ~ 48 centimeters with your left foot. Extend your fingers and put power in the palms of your hands. Then rotate them clockwise and counterclockwise several times.

After that, join your hands together and arch backwards as the dotted lines in the illustration show. Be sure to arch back as far as you can. This exercise can be difficult to get used to so initially do it 3 or 4 times before moving on to the next exercise.

Physical Education Exercise Step #3: Illustrated Explanation

This illustration shows how to place both hands on your hips and arch your body backwards.

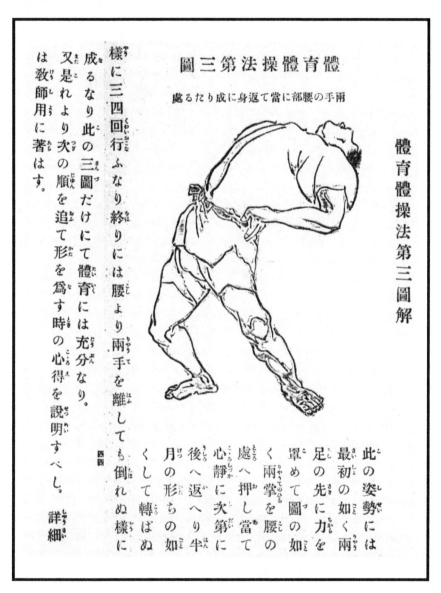

This illustration shows how to place both hands on your hips and arch your body backwards.

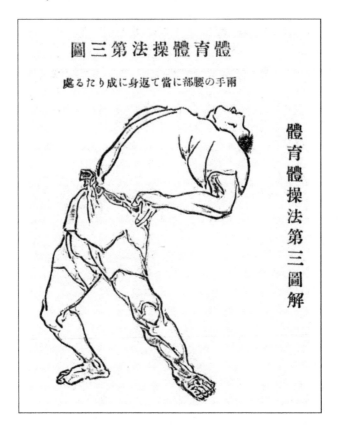

圖三第法操體育體

處るたり成に身返て當に部腰の手兩

體育體操法第三圖解

Physical Education Exercise Step #3: Illustrated Explanation

When beginning this exercise first put all your power in the ends of your toes. Then, as the illustration shows, place the palms of both hands on your waist. Calm your spirit at slowly push so that your arch back until your body is shaped like a crescent moon. Repeat this 3 or 4 times, being sure not to fall over.

Eventually you will be able to take your hands off your hips and arch back without falling. The exercise shown in Illustration 3 is quite effective even on its own.

In addition, I will also include the meaning and mindset you should have for all of the following techniques. You should consult your instructor for details on this.

262

Translator's Note:
All three exercises.

Step #1	Step #2	Step #3

Jujutsu Uchikomi : Illustrated Explanation

りな様む込打りよ勢姿の圖一第位之眞

This shows how you ready to strike.
Start from Shin no Kurai, True

柔術打込の圖解

Jujutsu Uchikomi : Illustrated Explanation

柔術家の打込と云ふは何流にても同じこと最初眞の位に立居より面前に敵あると假定して(エイ)と掛聲にて右手握り拳を以て前へ一足凡そ二尺迄の處へ右足を踏み出すと同時に振り上げて(ヤ丨と又掛聲にて打込なり。又元の所へ右足を引着けて元の八字形の位置となるなり。又打込む時は上に心ある故陰嚢を蹴られぬ様に左手を以て圖の如く陰嚢を圍むが定形なり。

Jujutsu Uchikomi : Illustrated Explanation
An Illustrated Description of How to Strike in Jujutsu

This section will introduce Uchikomi, or punching, done by Jujutsu practitioners. Uchikomi is done the same in all Jujutsu schools.

First, stand in Shin no Kurai, True Stance, and visualize an attacker standing in front of you. With a Kake-goe, or shout, of *Ei!* squeeze your right hand into a fist and take one step forward with your right foot. This step should be about 2 Shaku, 60 centimeters. At the same time you step, raise your right hand and strike with a Kake-goe of *Ya!*

Then return to your starting position. Pull your right foot back beside your left foot so your feet are in Hachimonji, open like the bottom of the Kanji for eight 八.

In addition, when you are striking, your attention is focused on the upper part of your body. Therefore, to protect against a kick to the "secret bag" or groin, keep your left hand cupped around your groin.

Jujutsu Katate Uke : Illustrated Explanation

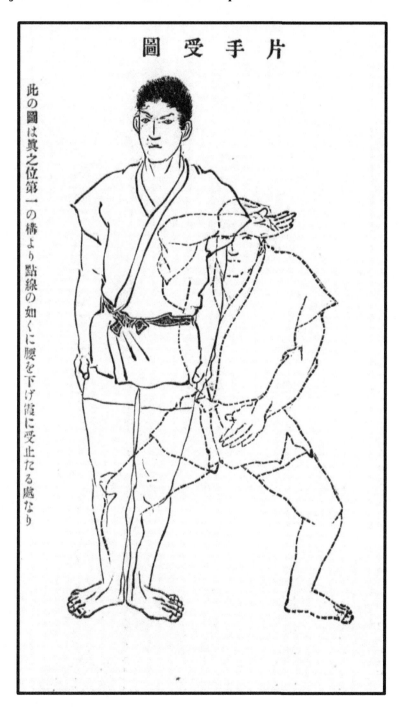

Jujutsu Katate Uke : Illustrated Explanation

柔術片手受の圖解

凡本圖の如く眞の位第一圖の通りに立ち即ち敵より右拳を以て打込み來たるを受ける構へなれば點線の如く第二眞之位の構へになるなり。右手掌を外に向けて前額に横一文字に當て受け留め同時に左足を横へ二尺位開き腰を下ろし下腹に力を罩め打込み來たる手首を摑るなり。

總て是は形に最も必要なり。元の如く直立して終るなり他に種種變化あるも形の書として後日著はす時詳細を説明す。

This illustration shows how you begin from Shin no Kurai, True Stance, #1, and then transition to a one-handed block.. As the dotted lines show, you have dropped your hips while raising your arm to block and stop the punch. The attacker is punching towards Kasumi, meaning mist, or the top of your head.

Jujutsu Katate Uke : Illustrated Explanation
How to Do a One-Handed Jujutsu Block

As the illustration shows, you are starting off in Shin no Kurai, True Stance #1.

An attacker punches you in the face with his right hand. The moment he begins his attack, take the stance shown by the dotted line. This stance is the second version of Shin no Kurai, or Shin no Kurai #2. The palm of your right hand should be held in front of your forehead, facing outward. Block the attacker's punch with your arm in Yoko Ichimonji, or held parallel to the ground in a straight line, at the same time step out to the side about 2 Shaku, 60 centimeters with your left foot. Drop your hips down and put power in your lower abdomen. After you block the attacker's punch grab his wrist.

The most important thing to learn in Jujutsu is Kata, or standard sets of movements with attacks and defenses. You return to the original upright stance after finishing this technique. There are many Henka, or variations, on this technique, and these will be explained in detail in a book of Kata I will release at a later date.[32]

---

[32] The author published the book *Complete Freedom to Kill or Resuscitate : A Guide to the Essene of Judo* 殺活自在柔道極意教範 in 1934, however it may have been available to instructors within the school before that.

Jujutsu Ryote Uke Tome : Illustrated Explanation

両掌を向に右手てし組合を受てし留腰

を下げて足を開きたる圖の構るたきなり

Jujutsu Ryote Uke Tome : Illustrated Explanation

柔術兩手受留の圖解

此の圖は敵より打ち込み來たる時に受くるの心得にて第一眞之

位の姿勢にて敵より打込まれたるものとして行ふ。敵が右手に

て打込み來たる時の受け方は兩手を圖の如くに組みて敵の眼を

兩手の下より見るやうに爲を定法とす。

同時に右足を後方斜に

二尺位の處へ開くなり。

又左手を以て打込み來たるときの受方は此の反對に行ふなり。

又左り足を引て開く事もあり是は敵の出方に依る者なり形に於

ては右手にて打が定式なり。

四八

271

腰留受てし合組を手てしに向を掌兩
りな圖の搆るたき開を足てげ下を

Block the attackers punch with the palms of both hands facing outwards and your hands crossed. The illustration shows how you should stand when blocking with your hips low and foot drawn back.

Jujutsu Ryote Uke Tome : Illustrated Explanation

This illustration shows how you defend against an opponent's punch with two hands. Initially, you are standing in Shin no Kurai #1 and then shift into this stance when the attacker punches.

Block the attacker's punch by crossing both hands as shown in the illustration. An important part of this technique is ensuring you can see the attacker from below your hands. At the same time step diagonally backwards 2 Shaku, 60 centimeters with your right foot.

In addition, if the attacker punches with his left hand, you should respond with your body in the opposite stance. What this means is you should drop diagonally backwards with your left foot. While the official way to do this technique is against a right punch, the way you respond depends on how the opponent attacks.

Jujutsu Kasumi Uchi Komi : Illustrated Explanation

Starting from the first illustration, strike with the end of your hand in a Shuto, Knife Hand, along the path of the dotted lines.

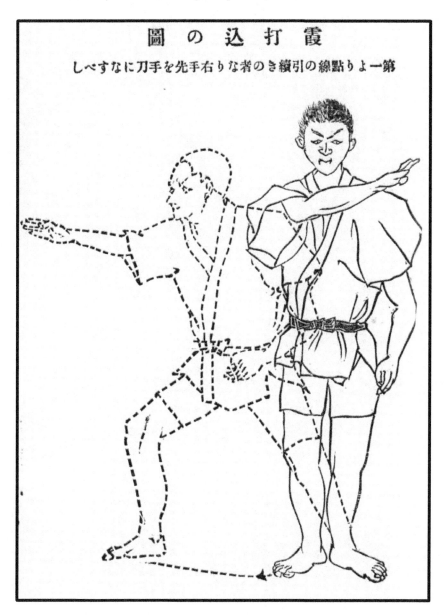

圖 の 込 打 霞

し べ す な に 刀 手 を 先 手 右 り な 者 の き 續 引 の 線 點 り よ 一 第

Jujutsu Kasumi Uchi Komi : Illustrated Explanation

柔術霞打込の圖解

此の圖も第一眞之位の位置にて起る者なり。前に敵あると假定して右手の五指を揃て手の側面にて敵の霞俗に蟀谷へ（當身の圖にある）と稱する處を目掛けて打つなり右手を點線の如くに爲し（エイ）と掛聲と共に右足を前に點線の如くに一歩踏み出すと同時に我が左肩口より斜に前へ向へ打込を定法とす。左手は右手足の出ると共に陰嚢を圍むべし。是れも形に必要なり。

正誤　此圖に點線の處は手先が今少上になる事と知らるべし

左手は今少下にあるがよしと知られたし。

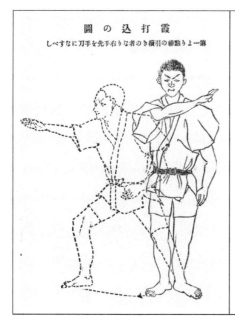

圖 の 込 打 霞

しべすなに刀手を先手右りな者のき横引の線點うよ一第

Starting from the first illustration, strike with the end of your hand in a Shuto, Knife Hand, along the path of the dotted lines.

Jujutsu Kasumi Uchi Komi : Illustrated Explanation

This strike also begins from Shin no Kurai, True Stance, #1. Imagine an opponent is in front of you. Join all the fingers of your right hand together and aim to strike with the side of your hand to the striking point known as Kasumi, or mist. This spot is also colloquially known as Komekami, valley of the crickets. (This is shown in the Atemi, or striking chart.) As you strike, shout a Kake-goe of *Ei!* Your right hand should follow the path indicated by the dotted line.

This is the proper way to do this strike to Kasumi. First step forward with your right foot, along the path indicated by the dotted line. At the same time swing your right arm from your left shoulder diagonally toward your target. This is shown by the dotted lines.

As you step forward with your right foot and strike with your right hand, your left hand should be protecting your Inno 陰嚢, "secret bag" or groin. This point is also important when doing Kata.

Small Correction: Be aware that the dotted lines in this illustration show the right hand slightly higher than what is ideal. In addition, be aware that it would be better if the left hand was slightly lower.

Jujutsu Tsuki Kake : Illustrated Explanation

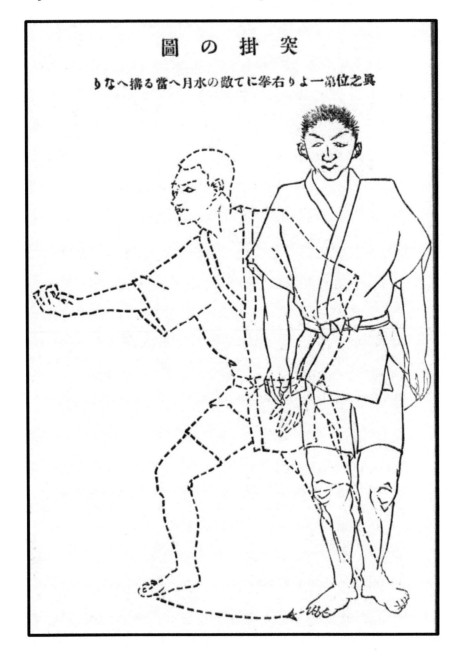

Jujutsu Tsuki Kake : Illustrated Explanation

柔術突掛の圖解

此の圖も前の霞と同じ樣なれ共只右手の違ふだけなり。

横腹に附け居る右拳を敵の水月に突き掛くる心得にて（エイ）と掛聲と共に手と同時に右足一歩前に進むなり。

拇指は中に折込で拳になすべきなり。是れも形に必要なり。後日教師用として著はす。

先に水月と云は當身の圖に明細にあり。

眞之位第一の構へより皆割出す處の者なればすべて此の柔術といふものは眞之位ほど大切の者と知るべし

277

圖 の 掛 突

As you can see, all these stances begin from Shinno Kurai #1. This should tell you how important this stance is in Jujutsu.

The Illustration show how you transition from Shin no Kurai #1 to strike your opponent in Suigetsu.

Translator's Note: Again, tucking the thumb inside the fingers was a common practice in early Japanese Jujutsu.

Jujutsu Tsuki Kake : Illustrated Explanation

The movement shown in this illustration is the same as in the previous one, Jujutsu Kasumi Uchi Komi. The only difference is the way the right hand strikes.

To strike with Tsuki Kake swing your right fist up from your side and , with a Kakegoe of *Ei!* strike the opponent in Suigetsu, light of the moon reflected on water, or the solar plexus. Step forward with your right foot the same time you strike.

Make a fist by folding your thumb inside your palm. This is also important when doing Kata. How to make a fist properly will be explained in greater detail the teacher's edition which will be released in the future.

For details regarding the Atemi point Suigetsu, please refer to the striking point and resuscitation chart.

Mukai Kaeri : Illustrated Explanation of a Front Roll #1

Begin from Shin no Kurai #2 and then transition to this position before rolling forward.

Mukai Kaeri : Illustrated Explanation of a Front Roll #2

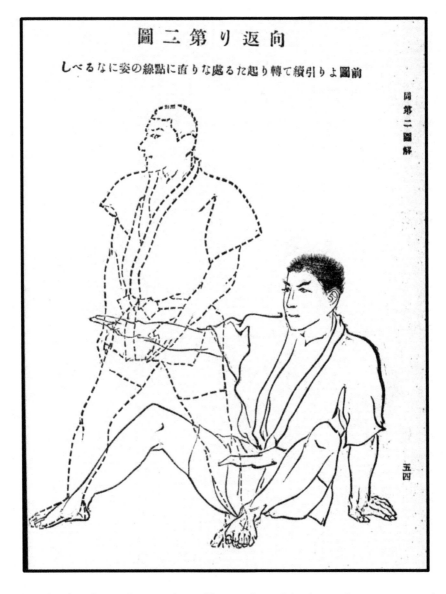

Continuing from the previous illustration, this shows how you stand up after. Adopt the stance shown by the dotted lines.

Mukai Kaeri : Illustrated Explanation of a Front Roll

向へ返り第一圖解

柔術向へ返りの第一圖解

此の形は最も必要なり。眞之位第二圖にて起り前を見て四つ這ひに斜に四肢を疊に着けて右足を眞前へ二尺斗り踏み出し同時に左手を疊に着け首を下げて自分の臍を賞める心持にて左足を上げて右肩を疊に着ける心持にて右手を疊に着けて向へ返る事直に引續き第二圖に移るなり。

同第二圖解

第一圖より轉ぶ時は右足前へ出で左足は曲げて左手は疊に着け右手は五指を揃へて横一文字に出すを定法とす。第一圖より引續き轉じたれば直に左手は陰嚢を圍み右手は右股に着け立ち上る迄三拍子引續きて行ふを定法とす絡らば元の眞之位第二の姿勢に成るべし。

五二

Mukai Kaeri : Illustrated Explanation of a Front Roll

Start	Step 1	Step 2	Finish
Begin from Shin no Kurai #2	*Transition to this position before rolling forward.*	*This shows how to stand up after your roll. Stand as shown by the dotted lines.*	*Finally, shift to Shin no Kurai #2.*

This is the most important Kata. Begin in Shin no Kurai, True Stance #2. While looking ahead, drop into a crawl aimed diagonally. First step straight ahead about 2 Shaku, 60 centimeters, and, at the same time, plant your left hand on the Tatami mat. It is important to tuck your chin and look towards your navel.

Raise your left leg and lower your right shoulder onto the Tatami. Place you right hand on the Tatami to help lower your body then roll over. The next step is shown in the following illustration.

At the end of the roll you began in Illustration #1, your right leg should be extended forward and your left knee bent. Your left hand should be flat on the Tatami mats and your right hand extended forward with your fingers pressed together. This standard arm positioning is called Yoko Ichi Moji, Straight Line Out to the Side.

After finishing the roll you began in the previous step, you should stand as shown by the dotted lines. Your left hand is protecting your groin and your right hand is on your right thigh. The proper timing for this technique is 3 beats : start, roll and stand up. Having finished you should return to Shin no Kurai #2.

Ushiro Kaeri : Illustrated Explanation of a Back Roll #1

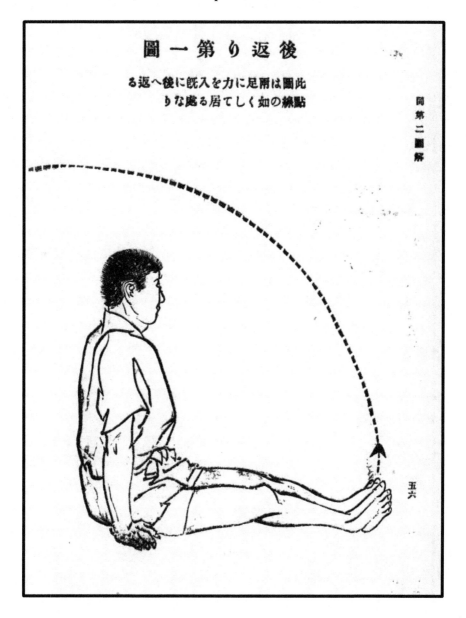

Ushiro Kaeri : Illustrated Explanation of a Back Roll #2

図二第り返後

前図より引き続き後へ返り背部右より見せたる處の図

Ushiro Kaeri : Illustrated Explanation of a Back Roll #3

Ushiro Kaeri : Illustrated Explanation of a Back Roll

柔術後返り第一圖解

此の返り方は修業上最も必要なり。眞之位第三圖より起り座し居る胸部を突かるゝ心持にて第一圖の如く兩足を揃へて右手にて疊を打ち同時に點線の如くにし次圖に移るなり。是に記す姿より點線の如くに兩足先に力を入兩手を疊を押附て頭より後へ返る氣になり右肩を疊に附て起る迄の事又都合にて左肩口より起るもあり。

同第二圖解

右手を以て疊を打ち足先に力を込め足先より順次後方へ返り足の爪先を疊に着けて元の姿勢となるを定法なりとす。第三圖を見て知らるべし。

此の處は兩足及び右肩を疊に着て左手を上に延し第壹圖より返りたる姿なり此は右側より返る處を見せたる處なり此の姿勢より直に眞之位第三の構へになるべし。

柔術後返り第一圖解

五五

Ushiro Kaeri : Illustrated Explanation of a Back Roll

Start	Step 1		
Shin no Kurai #3	Ushiro Kaeri #1	Ushiro Kaeri #2	Ushiro Kaeri #3

This is the most essential technique to learn during your Shugyo, or intensive training. It begins with you seated in Shin no Kurai #3, as if you have been knocked to the ground by a blow to the chest.

First, as Illustration #1 shows, bring your feet together. Next, strike the Tatami with your right hand as you raise your leges in the direction of the dotted lines. The moment continues in the next illustration.

When you begin this movement put power in your toes, push off the ground with both hands and move your legs along the path indicated by the dotted line. Roll back as if leading with your head, but your right shoulder should stay on the Tatami mat until you can stand. You will also have to roll over your left shoulder depending on the situation.

Strike the Tatami with your right hand as you put power into your toes. As your toes arc up, you rotate backwards until they touch the Tatami behind you. The technique is completed when you return to your original position. The explanation continues in Illustration #3.

This illustration shows your legs and right shoulder touching the Tatami. Your left arm is extended upwards. You have rolled back from the position shown in Illustration #1. These illustrations show how to roll backwards over your right shoulder.

At the end of the technique you should return to Shin no Kurai #3.

Ushiro Kaeri : Illustrated Explanation of a Back Roll

同第三圖解

後面のみにては解し難ければなり。

是れは第三圖の前面なり。

著者の親切を諒せられよ。

是處の姿勢は後へ返り左側より見たるなり必ず此姿になり毎日

稽古の時返る事を充分にして置時は亂捕又形の時は大意に廣得

をゐるなり。前にも云通り直に眞之位第三圖の構へになるべし。

終りを附ぬ時には極めが附ぬゆへ眞之位を以て定法となすべし。

This shows you from the front since it would be hard to explain if shown from just the back. This is an example of how kind the author is.

This shows you from the left after you have rolled backwards. It is important that you always end up in this position after rolling back. You should set aside time every training period to work on back rolls. It will offer many benefits when you are doing Randori, free sparring, or practicing Kata.

As was previously mentioned, when you finish immediately go into Shin no Kurai #3.

If you are unable to complete the back roll, that means you have yet to discover the secret how this technique is done. Nevertheless you should still stand up into Shin no Kurai #3 after your attempt.

Start	Step 1	Step 2
Begin from Shin no Kurai #3	*This illustration shows how you put power in your toes and roll back. Your feet should travel the path indicated by the dotted lines.*	*Continuing from the previous illustration, this shows your right side from the back as you roll over your right shoulder.*
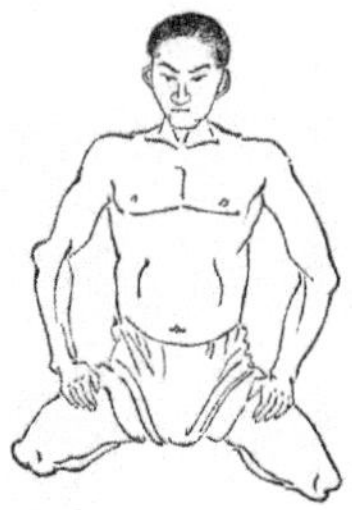	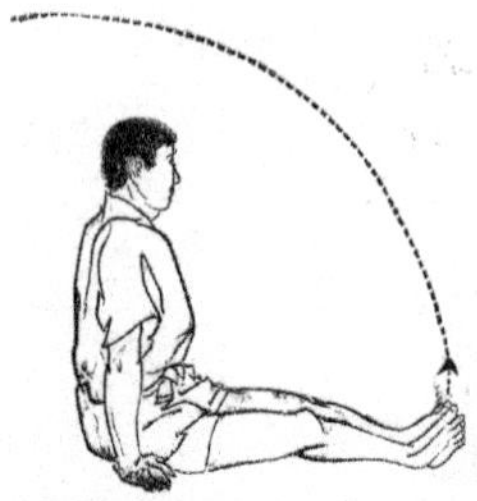	

Step 3	Finish
This shows the end of the roll from the front. This shows you from the front left.	*End in Shin no Kurai #3.*
	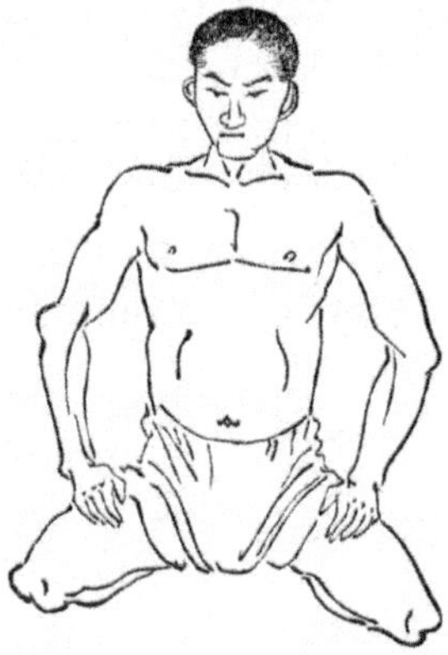

Overview of Handstands
Jujutsu no Sakadachi Keiko #1
Illustrated Explanation of Training Walking on Your Hands

逆立稽古の第一圖

兩掌を疊に附て向て既に
逆立せんとする處なり

是は兩足先に力を入て首を持
上ると業が好く出來る
なり。

同第二圖解

前の如くにして兩足を羽目板
に着けたる圖なり。此の樣に
して中心を保てば步行が掌に
て仕得る樣になるなり。

Jujutsu no Sakadachi Keiko #2
Illustrated Explanation of Training Walking on Your Hands

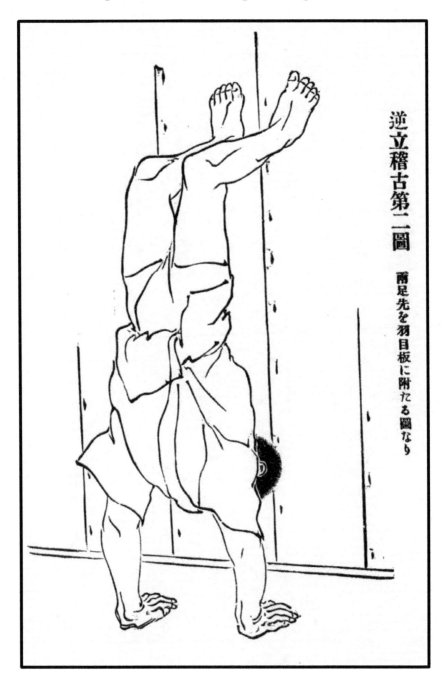

逆立稽古第二圖　兩足先を羽目板に附たる圖なり

Jujutsu no Sakadachi Keiko #3
Illustrated Explanation of Training Walking on Your Hands

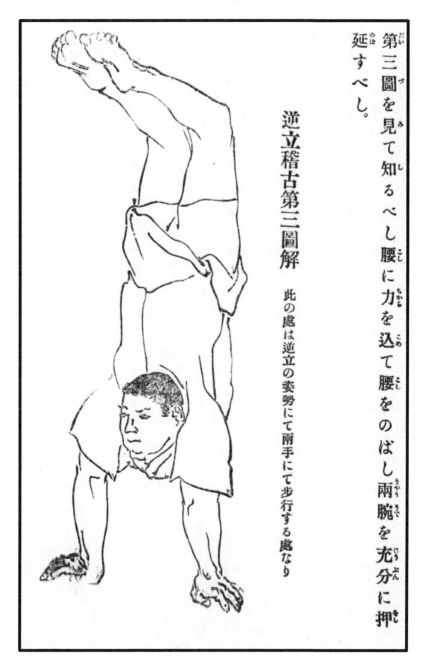

Explanation of Handstands
Jujutsu no Sakadachi Keiko #3
Illustrated Explanation of Training Walking on Your Hands

柔術逆立の稽古第一圖解

此の逆立と云ふは體育の上にも柔道練習の上にも大に必要なり。是れを學ぶには羽目板か又は柱の前方約二尺五六寸又は三尺位を隔つて立ち羽目際より一尺四五寸隔てし處へ兩手を疊に附けて横一文字に圖の如き姿勢になり首を上る同時に足先に力を罩めて跳ね上がり羽目板へ足を附けるなり。

Jujutsu no Sakadachi Keiko #1
Illustrated Explanation of Training Walking on Your Hands

Being able to do Sakadachi "Reverse Standing" or walking on your hands is essential not only for physical fitness but also in Judo Training.

To train this skill, stand in front of a wood paneled wall or column. You should position yourself between 2 Shaku and 5 or 6 Sun and 3 Shaku, 75 ~ 90 centimeters from the wall. Next, lean over and place your hands on the Tatami mats about 1 Shaku and 4 or 5 Sun, 42 ~ 45 centimeters, from the wall. Your arms should form Yoko Ichi Monji, or a straight line like the Kanji for the number one 一. The proper positioning is shown in the illustration.

Next, raise your head and put power in your toes. Push off the ground hard enough so that your feet contact the wall above you. The illustration shows how to put power in your toes and raise your neck. Doing this will allow you to execute a good handstand.

同第二圖解

前の如くにして兩足を羽目板に着けたる圖なり。此の樣にして中心を保てば歩行が掌にて仕得る樣になるなり。

第三圖を見て知るべし腰に力を込て腰をのばし兩腕を充分に押延すべし。

前の如くにして次第に馴れたれば兩掌にて歩行し得る樣になれば亂捕の稽古上甚だ德なり。何となれば敵に投げられし際兩手を疊に附け地上に體を落さざれはなり。昔の柔術家は指先二本にて逆立を爲したりと云ふ。

常に是を馴たる時は萬事に必用をかんずるなり。

296

Jujutsu no Sakadachi Keiko #2
Illustrated Explanation of Training Walking on Your Hands

Illustration 2	Illustration 3

This continues from the previous illustration. It shows your feet against the wall above you. If you are able to stabilize your core, you will be able to walk on the palms of your hands. As the following illustration shows, put power in your hips and stretch your hips while pushing with your harms as hard as you can.

Jujutsu no Sakadachi Keiko #3
Illustrated Explanation of Training Walking on Your Hands

If you practice as shown in the previous illustrations you will eventually become able to walk on your hands. This will be extremely beneficial to your Randori, free sparring. The reason is, when you get thrown by an opponent you can use your hands to contact the Tatami and prevent your body from hitting the ground. Long ago it is said that Jujutsu practitioners could do handstands using just two fingers on each hand.

If you make a habit of training this skill you will find it can be applied in a variety of situations.

Illustration 1

This shows how you begin a handstand. Your palms are on the ground and your back is moving up towards the wall.

Illustration 2	Illustration 3

This shows both your feet against the wall.

This show you in Sakadachi, walking on your hands.

Overview of Cartwheel
Jujutsu Kuruma Gaeri
Jujutsu Cartwheel Illustration 1

This illustration shows you ready to throw yourself to the side

圖一第り返車

りな處るすとんら返に横に既今は圖此

Jujutsu Kuruma Gaeri
Jujutsu Cartwheel Illustration 2

This illustration shows the person upside down, however the reader can adjust the way they view it to understand better. If your initial position is with your right hand up in the air, you should end up with your left hand in the air after finishing your cartwheel.

Jujutsu Kuruma Gaeri
Jujutsu Cartwheel Illustration 3

Beginning from two illustrations ago, you have rotated over and come up in this position.

車返り第三圖

前々より引續き第一二圖まできて直に起上りたるるたり圖るな り

Explanation of Cartwheels
Jujutsu Kuruma Gaeri
Jujutsu Cartwheel Illustration 1

柔術車返り第一圖解

此の車返りと云ふは練習上最も必要のものなり。是れを初心の内より稽古すれば體育上にも練習上にも身が輕くなりて投げらるゝ時には身體を地に落さず起き上るに早くして好都合なり。便利なり第一圖より二三と接續して一度のものと知るべし。元警視廳世話掛にて二級なりし故中村半助氏は良移心頭流の師範なりしが此人初心者には最初此の車返りを教へたりと云ふ第一圖の如く眞之位第二圖より起りて兩手を擴げ右手を圖の如く下

柔術車返り第一圖解

六三

Jujutsu Kuruma Gaeri
Jujutsu Cartwheel Illustration 1

The cartwheel is the most important thing you should train. When you get thrown during training, you can prevent your body from contacting the ground and return to a standing position by doing a cartwheel. This is very beneficial. If a beginner starts training cartwheels immediately he will become lighter and nimbler. This means he will be in better physical shape and perform better during training.

Be sure to study the progression of the illustrations, it is important to understand how illustrations 1,2 & 3 represent one set of movements.

The recently deceased Nakamura Hansuke(1845~1897), who was an instructor of Ryoi Shinto School[33], was heavily involved in the creation of the official Jujutsu curriculum for the Japanese police department. When new students started training the first thing he taught them was the cartwheel.

Begin this technique by standing in Shin no Kurai #2. As Illustration 1 shows, your arms are spread with your right arm angled down and your left arm angled up. Your legs are in Yoko Ichimonji, or spread apart in a straight line like the Kanji for one 一. The technique continues in the following illustration.

---

[33] The author indicates the name of this school can also be read as Rata Shinto School.

Jujutsu Kuruma Gaeri
Jujutsu Cartwheel Illustrations 2 & 3

左掌を地に附けて右手を疊に附けると同時に右足先に力を入れ第二圖の如くに爲して直に横に成るなり。

最も是れは順序を早くすべし腰業なれば第一圖より第二圖の如く兩手を擴げたるまゝ起き上る迄は唯腰だけの働なり。

是は總身を輕くして横へくゝと道場の廻りを數度なす時は次第に上達する最も亂捕には大必要なる事後に知るべし。

同第三圖解

第一圖より第二圖に至り此の三圖に於て壹手の形となるなり。

第一は左手を上にして第二圖になり此の起き上る圖になるなり

即ち第三圖は第一圖と反對に右手を上に左手を下になるなり

能く圖の手足の働き方に心を留めて勉むべし手を執りて教ふる

事能はざれば讀者熟讀して習ふべし。

Jujutsu Kuruma Gaeri
Jujutsu Cartwheel Illustration 2

First your left hand contacts the ground then your right hand makes contact with the Tatami mats. At the same time, put power in the toes of your right foot. You will then move into the position shown in illustration 2.

It is important to understand that the movements shown in the illustrations are done in rapid succession. A cartwheel is the product of Koshi-waza, or a technique that uses the hips. Starting at illustration 1, spreading your arms wide, then planting your hands on the ground and finally rotating over and returning to your starting position is all the result of the application of your hips.

This action will make your body light and by repeating the exercise around the Dojo several times, you will gradually become an expert. Later you will realize that this exercise is very important when doing Randori, free sparring.

Jujutsu Kuruma Kaeri
Jujutsu Cartwheel Illustration 3

Illustrations 1 ~ 3 show a single technique. In the first illustration you have your left hand up, in the second you have kicked your legs up, and in the final illustration you have your right hand up in the air. This is the mirror image of the starting position, so your left arm is down and your right arm is up.

Make sure you pay close attention to how the hands and feet are positioned in these illustrations. Since those learning by themselves do not have a teacher to instruct them, it is important to read the instructions closely.

Jujutsu Kuruma Gaeri
Jujutsu Cartwheel Illustrations 1 ~ 3

1	2	3

This illustration shows you ready to throw yourself to the side	*This illustration shows the person upside down, however the reader can adjust the way they view it to understand better. If your initial position is with your right hand up in the air, you should end up with your left hand in the air after finishing your cartwheel.*	*Beginning from two illustrations ago, you have rotated over and come up in this position.*

Overview of Jumping
Jujutsu Tobi-agari Keiko Zukai
An Illustrated Explanation of How to Train Your Vertical
Jump in Jujutsu
Illustration 1

Squeeze both your hands into fists and jump. This is how you should look when you do Issoku-tobi, jumping with both feet at the same time.

Jujutsu Tobi-agari Keiko Zukai
An Illustrated Explanation of How to Train Your Vertical Jump in Jujutsu
Illustration 2

This is Tobiagari, high jumping. You should put power in your toes and force them downward. You should land with both feet striking the ground at the same time.

Detailed Explanation of Jumping
Jujutsu Tobi-agari Keiko Zukai
An Illustrated Explanation of How to Train Your Vertical
Jump in Jujutsu Illustration 1

柔術飛上り稽古圖解

是は高く飛び上る事の稽古なり流儀に依れども昔は最初より飛

上りを教へたるものなり。　最初のうちは亂捕を教ふる前には必
七〇。

ず返り反り車返り、高飛を教へたるなり

柔術家としては體育上及柔術練習上必要なれば上達する樣稽古

を爲すべし。

高飛を爲すには第一圖の如く兩手の拇指を掌の中に折り込み兩

足を爪立ち爪先に力を入れ口を結びて下腹に力を罩め身を輕く

し飛ぶ心得なり。

廣き地所の有處にて二尺斗の高さの土堤を築き又其上に罌粟種

を蒔て次第に延るにしたがい高く飛べる樣になり朱。順次三尺

余にのびる時は五尺余も飛上る事が充分に出來る事あり。

Jujutsu Tobi-agari Keiko Zukai
How to Train Your Vertical Jump in Jujutsu   Illustration 1

Squeeze both your hands into fists and jump. This is how you should look when you do Issoku-tobi, jumping with both feet at the same time.

This next section will look at how to train your vertical jump so that you can jump high. Long ago, jumping was the first thing taught in many schools of Jujutsu, though it did vary from school to school. Before engaging in Randori, free sparring, lessons in front rolls, back rolls, cartwheels and vertical jumping were taught.

Being an expert at jumping high is necessary not only for Jujutsu practitioners but also your physical fitness and Jujutsu training.

The way to do Taka-tobi, high jumping, training begins in illustration 1. First tuck your thumbs against your palms and then wrap your fingers over them. Stand on your toes and focus all your power there. Close your mouth and put power in your lower abdomen, and focus on making your body feel light as you jump up. If you have a wide area, make a mound of earth about 2 Shaku, 60 centimeters, tall. Then plant some poppy seeds on top of that mound. The plants will gradually grow taller and you will become able to jump higher. Eventually the plants will grow to and the height will be 3 Shaku, 90 centimeters. Later, though the total height will be closer to 5 Shaku, 150 centimeters, you will still be able to jump over it.

Jujutsu Tobi-agari Keiko Zukai
An Illustrated Explanation of How to Train Your Vertical Jump in Jujutsu Illustration 2

同第二圖解

兩足を縮めて飛び上り下る際は爪先を揃へ身を輕くして下るなり。此圖は飛上りたる處なり初心のものは最初二尺位の土手を築き其上に芥子の種を蒔き次第に延て花の咲くころ凡そ二尺ほどゝなりし上を花に觸れぬ樣に次第に稽古する内に身も輕くなるなり。自宅又は道場にて爲す時は紐にて圖の如く二尺位より次第に高くすべし終には四尺五尺と高く飛ぶ樣になるべし。

312

Jujutsu Tobi-agari Keiko Zukai
How to Train Your Vertical Jump in Jujutsu   Illustration 2

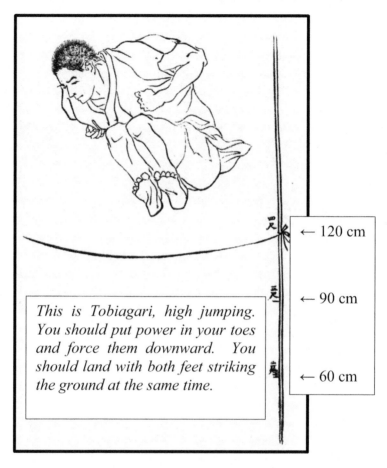

This is Tobiagari, high jumping. You should put power in your toes and force them downward. You should land with both feet striking the ground at the same time.

← 120 cm

← 90 cm

← 60 cm

Tense your legs and then jump up. When you land, keep your feet together and land lightly on the balls of your feet. This illustration shows how you jump up. Beginners should build a mound of earth about 2 Shaku tall and then plant poppy seeds on top. As the plants grow, continue to jump over them, ensuring your feet do not touch the flowers. By doing this kind of training your body will become lighter. If you want to do this kind of training at home or at the Dojo, you can use a piece of string. Then, as the illustration shows, gradually increase the height. Eventually, you will become able to jump over a string tied at 4 or 5 Shaku, 120 ~ 150 centimeters.

How to Grab and How to Choke
Illustrated Explanation :
Grabbing the Collar With Your Right Hand & Reverse Grip

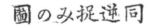

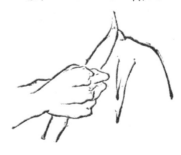

圖のみ捉逆同

圖るたみ捉を襟右

右襟の取り様の圖解

右襟を取るときは小指より紅指と順に力を入れ人指指は軽く握ること總じて襟を取る時は、拇指と小指に力を入るゝが定法と知るべし。

同逆の圖解

右襟を逆に取るには拇指を外部に現はし圖の如く爲すなり。此手は形及絞めに用ふるなり。亂捕の時は成るべく逆手は用ひざるが宜し。

左襟の取り様の圖解

Illustrated Explanation :
Grabbing the Collar With Your Right Hand

When taking your opponent's collar with your right hand, grip first with your pinky and then with your ring finger. Your index finger should always grip lightly. The standard way of gripping the collar is to put power into your little finger and thumb.[34]

Illustrated Explanation:
Grabbing the Collar With Your Right Hand in a Reverse Grip

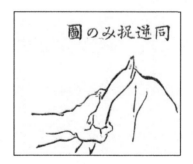

When taking your opponent's collar with a right reverse grip, your thumb will be on the outside as shown in the illustration. This way of grabbing is used both in Kata training and when doing Shime, or chokes. It is best not to use Gyakute, or a reverse grip, during Randori.

---

[34] The author refers to this as Migi-Eri, right collar, but this means "grabbing your opponent's left collar with your right hand."

Illustrated Explanation :
Grabbing the Collar With Your Left Hand & Reverse Grip

圖のみ捉逆同　　圖るたみ捉を襟左

一二

左襟の取り様の圖解

右と別に違ひなし唯左襟を左手にて捉みたるだけなり。敵の襟を取るには双方共に肩より下四五寸の處を捉むを定法とすれども人には身體の大小其他の都合もあれば必ず其れとは定ず其場合に臨み定法に大差なき程度にて取ること丶心得べし。

同逆の圖解

右の逆の反對なり他に變る所なし摑み處の名稱は左右襟帶、袖口、上下八ツ口等は一定の捉む所なり形、亂捕等は總て以上の所を摑みて種々の業を施すなり。

Illustrated Explanation : How to Grab the Collar With Your Left Hand

This grab is the same as with the right hand. The only difference is that you are grabbing with the left. No matter which side of your opponent's Eri, or collar, you grab, the proper spot is about 4 or 5 Sun, 12 ~ 15 centimeters below the shoulder. However, since people vary in sizes this is not a hard-fast rule. You will have to adjust the distance to a degree when training.

Illustrated Explanation : How to Grab the Collar With Your Left Hand in a Reverse Grip

This is exactly the same as the right reverse grip but with your left hand. Some of the names of the standard places to grab are:
Sayu Eri : Left and Right Collar
Sayu Obi : Left and Right Belt
Sayu Sode Guchi : Left and Right End of the Sleeve
Ue Yatsu Kuchi : Upper Opening in the Armpit
Shita Yatsu Kuchi : Lower Opening in the Armpit.
You will employ all these different grabs when doing Kata training or Randori.

Illustrated Explanation : How to Grab the Belt With a Regular and Reverse Grip

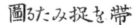

圖るたみ捉に逆を帶　　　圖るたみ捉を帶

帶捉み處の圖解

八〇

都而柔道稽古の時は帶は必ず前にて結ぶべし。是れは結び目が後にては仰向に倒れし時危險なればなり。

摑み方は袖襟同樣に握り前後左右を圖の如く摑むなり。

同逆捉みの圖解

逆と云ふは掌を上に向け摑むを逆と云ふ掌を下に向け摑むを順と云ふなり。解り易ければ説明の用なし。是は掌が下になり居るは誤なり。

喉緒の圖解

Illustrated Explanation : How to Grab the Belt

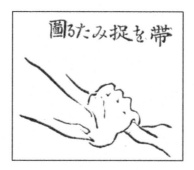

Always tie your belt in the front when you are doing Jujutsu training. If you fall backwards with your belt tied on your back, it would be extremely dangerous.

You grab the belt the same way you grab the collar or sleeve. Grab left, right, front or back as shown in the illustration.

Illustrated Explanation : How to Grab the Belt With a Reverse Grip

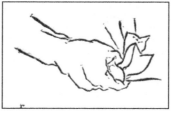

In Jujutsu the word Gyaku means the palm of your hand is facing up when you grab. When you grab with your palm facing downward it is called Jun. Since this is a pretty simple concept I need not elaborate further. This illustration showing your palm facing down is an error.

Illustrated Explanation : Nodo Shime Throat Choke

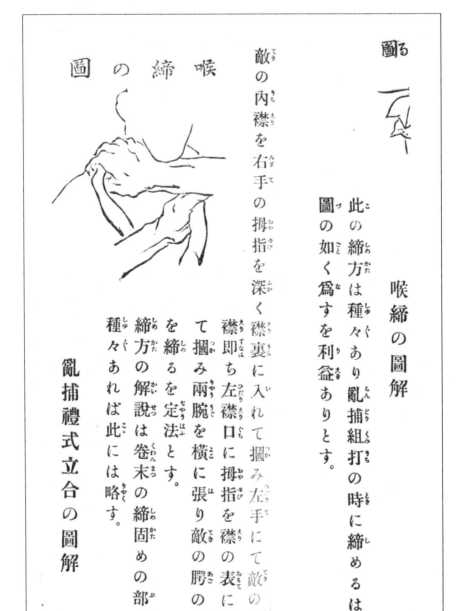

圖る

喉締の圖解

此の締方は種々あり亂捕組打の時に締めるは
圖の如く爲すを利益ありとす。

喉締の圖

敵の内襟を右手の拇指を深く襟裏に入れて摑み左手にて敵の上
襟即ち左襟口に拇指を襟の表にして摑み兩腕を横に張り敵の膈の下
を締るを定法とす。
締方の解説は卷末の締固めの部に
種々あれば此には略す。

亂捕禮式立合の圖解

Illustrated Explanation : Nodo Shime Throat Choke

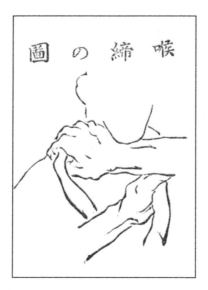

There are many different ways to do this choke. When doing Randori or pair training the choke shown in the illustration is the most effective one to apply.

Grab the opponent's Uchi Eri, or collar near the throat, by pushing your thumb deep under his collar. Your left hand grabs his Uwa Eri, or collar on the left side. Grip you're your left thumb on the outside of his collar. The standard way to apply this choke is to pull outward with both arms so your opponent's shirt is pulled tight under his jaw.

Chokes will be explained at the end of this volume in the chapter titled Shime Katame, so the explanation will be abbreviated here.

柔　術　教　科　書

柔術締絞業解説

此の締絞業は固業よりも危險にて締めて居る内に相手がいつか呼吸が止り居ることあり故に人工呼吸術又は活法にて蘇生せしむるなり。

上達してより締業を用ふるは自由なれども初心の者は教師及先輩の者の同席無き時は逆手締業は掛けざる様心得べし。昔の柔術界にては逆締等最も流行せしも現今は一般に投業を專門とする傾向なれども流儀に依りて締逆を專門に教へる所もあるなり他流と組討をする時は先づ逆又締業を以て施す是を受る心得が無くては如何と思ひ著す者と知るべし。

Jujutsu Shime Shibari Waza Kaisetsu
An Explanation of Chokes and Strangling Techniques[35]

Chokes and Strangling techniques are more dangerous that joint locks. You cannot predict when a person being choked is going to stop breathing, thus it is important to be able to use artificial breathing techniques as well as striking resuscitation points.

Once you become adept at Shime Waza you will have complete freedom to use those techniques, however beginners should not attempt Gyakute Shime Waza, reverse hand chokes, unless the Sensei or another instructor is present. Long ago, Jujutsu practitioners focused on Nage Waza, Throwing Techniques, as opposed to the Reverse Hand Chokes that are practiced extensively today.

However, there were certain schools that specialized in Shime Gyaku, Reverse Hand Chokes. Whenever you visit another school to spar, the first thing you should do is apply Gyaku, joint locks, or Shime Waza, Chokes. If they do not seem to be familiar with the techniques this should be a red flag regarding that school.

---

[35] This section on choke holds actually appears later in the book, but I decided to include it here so that all the information related to chokes is together.

Jujutsu Juji Shime Zukai
Illustrated Explanation : Cross Shaped Choke

柔　術　敎　科　書

十　字　絞　圖

此の寫生本文にて知るべし今既に首を
さげて指先より充分に手が掛たるゆ
ゑに締かるを處見せたる者なり

Pay close attention to what is being shown in this illustration. You have already taken hold of his collar on both sides of his neck and are putting power into your fingertips. This shows you in the final stage of applying the choke.

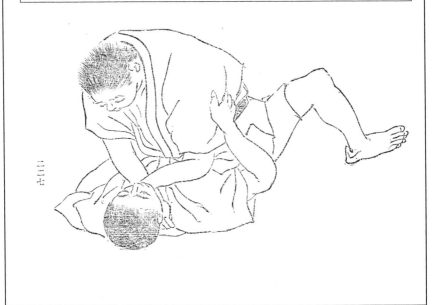

324

Jujutsu Juji Shime Zukai
Illustrated Explanation : Cross Shaped Choke

柔術雙絞十字圖解

是は相手が仰向に倒れたる腹の上に馬乗りになり。兩膝頭を疊に附けて兩足先を爪立て臀を相手の臍に押當右手にて左肩の襟を握り左手は右肩襟の處を同じく小指より順次に力を入れて攔み咽喉に我が顔を少しく横に向けて兩肘を張り總身に力を込めて十文字に締る時は必ず相手は締められて假死するなり。是れを外し逃るゝには相手が兩肘を疊に附けて締附る迄に下より兩掌を以て相手の兩臂頭を押上ぐと同時に下腹及兩足先に力を罩めて跳ね除けるなり。

襟を深く取りたる時は腕先にても締めらるゝも淺く取りし時は兩臂を疊に附くるまでに絞るべし。

三二八

Pay close attention to what is being shown in this illustration. You have already taken hold of his collar on both sides of his neck and are putting power into your fingertips. This shows you in the final stage of applying the choke.

Jujutsu Juji Shime Zukai
Illustrated Explanation : Cross Shaped Choke

This choke begins after your opponent has fallen on his back. You are on his stomach in Uma-nori, or mounting him like a horse. Your kneecaps should be on the Tatami along with the toes of your feet. Your butt should be on top of the opponent's navel, pressing down. Your right hand grabs the opponent's right collar near his shoulder and your left hand grabs his left collar near his shoulder. Put power in your fingers starting with your little finger. The opponent's throat should be slightly to the side of your face. Focus your power in your elbows and use all the power in your body to choke.

Once you apply a Juji Shime, your opponent will almost immediately fall into a state of Kashi, Near-Death (unconsciousness.) In order to escape this choke the opponent should plant both his elbows on the ground and work his hands around until he can grab both your elbows from below. With his hands cupping the elbows he should then put power in his legs and lower abdomen and shove upward as if trying to jump up.

If you grab deep when applying this choke, you can use your forearms to choke. If your grab is shallow pull outwards until your elbows touch the Tatami mats.

Jujutsu So-Juji Shime Zukai
Illustrated Explanation : Simultaneous Cross Shaped Choke

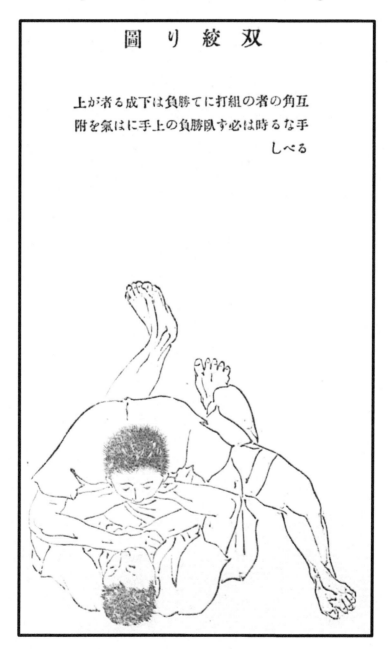

Jujutsu So-Juji Shime Zukai
Illustrated Explanation : Simultaneous Cross Shaped Choke

柔術雙十字絞圖解

上なる者は兩膝を突き居る時は横に倒され易き故圖の如く左片足先に力を入れて立膝を爲すなり。此の圖は下の方が充分に手が取りあれば下の方の者に勝ある様に見ゆるも上の者が七分の徳あり上の者は下より締られ又は跳飛されぬ様にするなり。上にても下にても充分に締めたる時は樂なる方へ顔を横に向けて居るべし。

Regarding bouts where you and your opponent are of equal skill: If the person who ends up on the bottom is more skilled at Fuse Shobu, Battling on the Ground, you should be careful when you are mounted and trying to apply a choke.

Jujutsu So-Juji Shime Zukai
Illustrated Explanation : Simultaneous Cross Shaped Choke

If the person on top has both knees on the ground, then it is easy to topple him to the side. Thus, as the illustration shows, the left leg of the man on top is out to the side bracing his body. As the illustration shows, if you are on the bottom you still have an opportunity to win by putting on a choke of your own. That being said the person on top has a 70% greater chance of achieving a better choke than the person below. The person on the bottom can also throw the other person off to the side.

It doesn't matter if you are on the top or on the bottom, when you are applying the choke, turning your face to the side will make the technique easier.

Ayakotei
Illustrated Explanation : Rope Pattern Choke

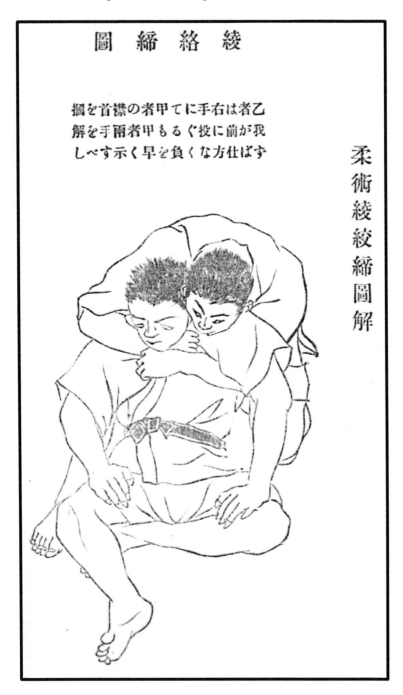

圖　綟　絡　綾

乙は者右手にて甲の者襟首を搦を
我が前に投ぐるも甲者兩手を解を
す仕方なく負を早く示すべし解を

柔術綾綟絞綟圖解

Ayakuri Shime
Illustrated Explanation : Rope Pattern Choke

我は相手の背に廻り右手にて相手の左襟元を取り左手は左脇下へ差入れて相手の右肩口の稽古衣を摑みて左膝を疊に突て足の爪先を立て居るなり。右足は立膝を爲して頭をば相手の左肩へ押附けて兩臀を張り總身に力を罩めて締るなり。此の手に掛りたる時は逃るゝ術なければ速に賔を示すべし。

Ayakuri Shime
Illustrated Explanation : Rope Pattern Choke

Move around so you are behind your opponent. Grab high on his left collar with your right hand. Thread your left hand under his left armpit, then reach across his chest and grab his Keikogi on his right shoulder. Plant your left knee on the Tatami mat but just the toes of your left foot, so your heel is off the ground.

Keep your right foot planted on the ground, with your knee pushing into your opponent's right shoulder. Focus your strength in your elbows as you force them outward using your whole body.

If someone applies this technique on you, unless you have a ready escape, you should tap out quickly.

Ayakotei
Illustrated Explanation : Rope Pattern Choke

圖　締　絡　綾

If the person defending reaches back with his right hand and grabs the attacker's collar near his neck, the defender can throw him forward. This will force the attacker to release his grip and he will have to quickly signal his defeat.

柔術綾絞締圖解

Migi Ushiro Karami
Illustrated Explanation : Back Right Tangle

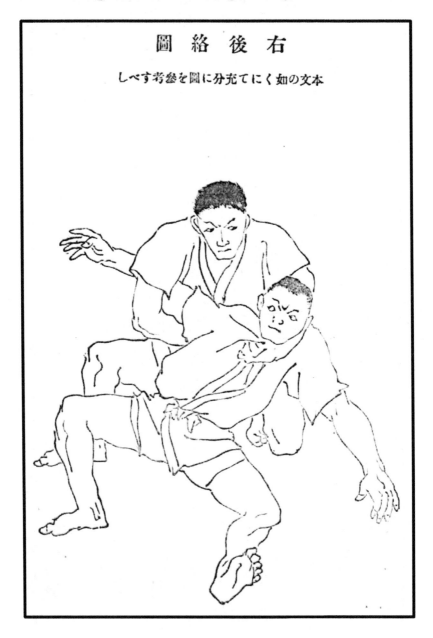

圖 絡 後 右

本文の如くにて充分に圖を参考すべし

Migi Ushiro Karami
Illustrated Explanation : Back Right Tangle

柔術右後絡圖解

我れ相手の背部に廻り右腕にて相手の右胸を外より巻き込み手先にて稽古衣の紋所を逆に摑み左手は可成相手の左脇の下へ寄り右肩口の襟を取るべし。然して左足を大きく後方へ引いて膝を突くと自然に相手の體が崩れて後方へ倒るゝなり。其時に右膝を立て下腹に力を罩めて兩手先を以て締るなり。乙者は前と同じ。

Follow the written instructions and study this illustration carefully.

Migi Ushiro Karami
Illustrated Explanation : Back Right Tangle

Move behind your opponent and wrap your right arm forward towards his chest before wrapping it around his right arm. Grab the back of his Keikogi in the center, where the family crest would go. Your hand will be gripping Gyaku, or palm up. Your left hand should move from below your opponent's left shoulder and reach across to his right shoulder. Grab his Keikogi there.

As you do this take a large step back with your left leg and plant your knee on the ground. This will naturally cause your opponent to lose his balance and fall backwards. You should keep your right leg upright and put power in your lower abdomen and choke the opponent by pulling. The power should go in your fingertips first. The opponent should resist in the same way as mentioned previously.[36]

---

[36] *If the person defending reaches back with his right hand and grabs the attacker's collar near his neck, the defender can throw him forward. This will force the attacker to release his grip and he will have to quickly signal his defeat.*

Hidari Ushiro Karami
Illustrated Explanation : Back Left Tangle

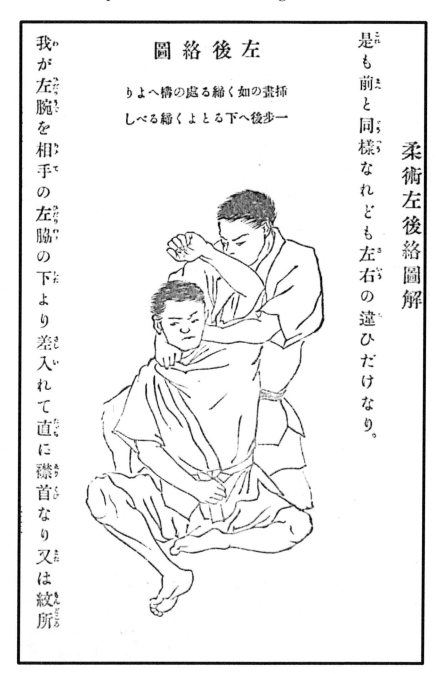

圖 絡 後 左

りよへ槽の處る締く如の畫挿
しべる締くよとる下へ後歩一

是も前と同様なれども左右の違ひだけなり。

柔術左後絡圖解

我が左腕を相手の左脇の下より差入れて直に襟首なり又は紋所

Hidari Ushiro Karami
Illustrated Explanation : Back Left Tangle

柔術左後絡圖解

是も前と同様なれども左右の違ひだけなり。

我が左腕を相手の左脇の下より差入れて直に襟首なり又は紋所の處を早く取り右手を以て左肩の襟元を取り圖の如くし直に左足を大きく後へ引きて膝を突き立て足先を爪立て右膝を立て同時に兩手先にて締るなり。

前圖及此圖は讀者の解し易き爲に肩口より寫生したり。

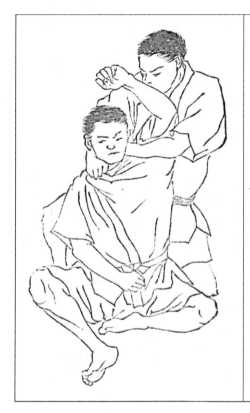

This illustration shows how you should be positioned for this choke. Note that you will get a better choke if you take one step backwards.

Hidari Ushiro Karami
Illustrated Explanation : Back Left Tangle

This technique is the same as the previous one, except that it is done on the left instead of the right.

Your left arm should slide under your opponent's left armpit and towards the back of his neck. Then quickly grab his Keikogi in the center of his back, where the family crest would go. Your right hand should grab his left Eri-moto, the top of his collar, as shown in the illustration.

Then pull your left leg back a big step and drop onto your left knee while keeping your right leg upright. The toes of your left foot should be on the ground with your heel up. At the same time choke with both hands. This illustration, as well as the previous one, are shown from the front so you can see how the hands are on the shoulders.

Hadaka-toh
Illustrated Explanation : Naked Lock

Hadaka-toh
Illustrated Explanation : Naked Lock

柔術裸體捕圖解

此の裸體捕と云ふは手數種々あれども今は其の一を説くべし。

他は之を應用したるなり理は同じと知るべし。

我は相手の背部に廻り直に右腕を右肩口より咽喉に掛け左腕を左肩へ掛け掌を以て相手の後頭部を押へ右掌にて我が二の腕を握りて相手の身體を我が胸の處へ引附ると同時に腰は其儘にて大きく左右足を後方へ引き下ると共に左掌を向へ押附ければ相手は此れを解く術なく咽喉を締め附けられ早く頁を示すべし。

左右とも能く利く捕方なれば勝手宜き方を早く掛るべし。

是は稽古衣ぬけて裸體になる時の形なり又眞揚流に裸身捕と云三種の形にもあり.

是れは如何しても解く事のできん形なるゆへためして見るべし。

亂捕の形は此位にして置又教師用には成丈明細に記べし。

This is how you apply the Naked Lock. You should study this illustration carefully.

Hadaka-toh
Illustrated Explanation : Naked Lock

This technique is known as Hadaka-toh, Naked Lock. While there are a great number of variations on this technique, the one I will introduce here will allow you to use the other versions as well since the underlying principle is the same.

Approach the opponent from the back and immediately reach over his right shoulder and wrap your arm around his throat. Reach over his left shoulder with your left arm. Place the palm of your left hand on the back of your opponent's head and push. The palm of your right hand grips your left bicep. Pull the opponent's body towards your chest and, at the same time take big steps back with your left and right legs. As you do this push your left palm forward. If you opponent does not have a technique to escape this then he will be choked, thus he should quickly indicate he is defeated.

This technique is equally effective with either the right arm first or the left arm first so the person applying the technique should rapidly apply the technique on whichever side is easiest in that situation.

This technique is used when you remove your Keiko-I and train naked. There are also three Hadaka-toh, Naked Lock, techniques in the Shinyo school.

This is just an explanation of how to do this choke. You should try this technique during your training. This is the end of the section on Randori techniques, there will be more extensive explanations in the forthcoming instructor's guide.

A Collection of Curious Jujutsu Manuals Volume 3
End

Printed in Great Britain
by Amazon

24044609R00195